The Practical, Moral, and Personal Sense of Nursing

The Practical, Moral, and Personal Sense of Nursing

A Phenomenological Philosophy of Practice

Anne H. Bishop
John R. Scudder, Jr.

State University of New York Press

Excerpt from "Little Gidding" in *Four Quartets*, copyright 1943 by
T.S. Eliot and renewed 1971 by Esme Valerie Eliot, reprinted by permission
of Harcourt Brace Jovanovich, Inc.

Published by
State University of New York Press, Albany
©1990 State University of New York

For information, address State University of New York
Press, State University Plaza, Albany, N.Y., 12246
Library of Congress Cataloging-in-Publication Data

Bishop, Anne H., 1935-
    The practical, moral, and personal sense of nursing : a
phenomenological philosophy of practice / Anne H. Bishop, John R.
Scudder, Jr.
        p.   cm.
    Bibliography: p.
    Includes index.
    ISBN 0-7914-0251-7. — ISBN 0-7914-0252-5 (pbk.)
    1. Nursing—Psychological aspects. 2. Nursing—Moral and ethical
aspects.   I. Scudder, John R., 1926—.   II. Title.
    [DNLM: 1. Nursing. 2. Philosophy. Nursing.   WY 86 B622p]
    RT86.B46   1990
    610.73'01—dc20
    DNLM/DLC
    for Library of Congress   89–11480
                                                                    CIP

10 9 8 7 6 5 4 3 2 1

Contents

Acknowledgments

There are various ways in which others contribute to a work like this. There are direct contributions through which scholars read and make recommendations which improve the work. There are historical contributions which evoke the work and foster its development. There are institutional contributions which give monetary and release time support. Finally, there are personal contributions in the form of encouragements and of freeing scholars from mundane activities.

Patricia Benner and Richard Zaner read earlier versions of this book and made many helpful criticisms. In addition, they shared versions of books on which they were working which contributed to this work. Joseph Freeman III read the entire manuscript, some portions of it several times, to help improve its style and clarity. Thomas Brickhouse assisted us in working through certain portions of the book, especially those related to Aristotle.

Initially, our informal conversations concerning health care and phenomenological philosophy were focused by the work of and especially conversations with three scholars. Algis Mickunas helped us understand phenomenology in a way that could be readily related to health care. Edmund Pellegrino reversed this direction by giving us an interpretation of health care which was amenable to phenomenological articulation. Richard Zaner helped us put both together. This thought began to take form when we directed a conference and edited a book entitled *Caring, Curing, Coping:*

Nurse, Physician, Patient Relationships. Anna-Teresa Tymieniecka actually initiated this work by asking us to write
an extensive article concerning the moral sense of health
care for her publication, *The Analecta Husserliana*, and
further contributed to it by encouraging us to deliver papers
at her conferences. We are also indebted to the Society for
Phenomenology and the Human Sciences and the Human
Science Research Conference for encouraging and fostering
the kind of work that we do. Throughout our research we
have found many nurses who were willing to share their
thoughts and stories concerning the practice of nursing, and
we are especially indebted to them for helping to make this
work concrete.

We are indebted to Lynchburg College, especially the
Faculty Research and Development Committee, for sabbati-
cal leaves and many grants which made this publication
possible. Also we are indebted to the Virginia Foundation for
Humanities and Public Policy for supporting the conference
and publication on Caring, Curing and Coping.

We are grateful to the faculty of Lynchburg College for
giving us a collegial atmosphere in which to work. We very
much appreciate the friendship, encouragement, and support of our colleagues in the departments of philosophy and
nursing, especially our chairs, Ronald Martin and Barbara
Whitmeyer, for their support. We are especially grateful for
the many ways in which our spouses, Mary and Bobby, have
encouraged and supported us during the writing of this
book.

Chapter 1

Introduction

The development of a philosophy of nursing has been surprisingly slow in the United States when one considers the rapid advances of nursing in hospital, community, and higher education settings. With the development of baccalaureate, masters, and doctoral programs in nursing, scholars in nursing have attempted to articulate their discipline and set it in a broader cultural context. Some scholars have looked outside of nursing to the natural or behavioral sciences for models with which to articulate the practice of nursing as an academic discipline. In so doing, nursing is following a trend in contemporary higher education, but unlike other practice-disciplines, they have not developed philosophical treatments of their practice-discipline as have medicine and education, for example. Traditionally in the West, articulation of a human activity within a broad cultural context has been accomplished by those philosophies called "philosophy of x." Although in the past philosophy has been neglected in nursing education, many nurses are becoming more familiar with philosophy as a result of the current emphasis on ethics in nursing. But as yet, development of a philosophy of nursing is still in its infancy. We believe that the time is right for a philosophical articulation of nursing.

Our own interest in the philosophy of nursing did not begin with the discovery of a vacuum in academic nursing, i.e., a concern that this field has been neglected by scholars and needed to be "developed." Our conviction came from

1

years of dialogue between nurse-educator and philosopher. The nurse (Bishop) found in continental philosophy (phenomenology, existentialism, and hermeneutics) a way of thinking about nursing which brought together the emphasis on practice from her hospital experience and the stress on improving nursing through a more adequate understanding of it from her academic experience. The philosopher (Scudder) experienced the excitement of having philosophy related to the world as it had been when he first began articulating education philosophically. He had come to believe, with many of his veteran colleagues, that philosophy of education was becoming an ingrown specialty in which philosophers of education spoke to each other rather than to practicing educators. Both partners found their dialogue productive, exciting, and surprising. Scudder was amazed to find himself entering a new field of endeavor late in his career after completing a phenomenological philosophy of education which was the culmination of many years in both fields. Bishop was also astounded that after a long career in nursing, including nursing education in both hospital and collegiate settings, she was seeking and finding in philosophy new insights into issues in nursing which had long troubled her, especially since she had previously regarded philosophy as irrelevant to nursing practice. Since this book grew out of a dialogue rather than a decision to enter a new academic specialty, it is neither an attempt to introduce nurses to phenomenological philosophy nor a survey of a few previous attempts to treat nursing philosophically. Instead, it is our attempt to share our dialogue with a wider audience, drawing on the philosophers and scholars of nursing who have spoken most forcefully to us.

Perhaps the slow development of a philosophy of nursing has resulted from the belief, like that formerly held by Bishop, that philosophical interpretations are inappropriate to concrete practices like nursing. Those whose only experience of philosophy was in a traditional introductory course often tend to believe that philosophy is an abstract treatment of the world which is applied to anyone, any situation, at any time. This caricature of philosophy is not without some justification, however. The philosopher, Martin Heidegger, did criticize the Western philosophical tradition for its failure to be concrete and rooted in everyday experience. He attributed this lack to a general tendency in our society to prefer calculative thinking over meditative thinking. Calculative thinking is the type of thinking which permeates the natural and social sciences and the technologies which they have spawned. Heidegger was aware that practical people tended to be suspicious of meditative thinking.

> Yet you may protest: mere meditative thinking finds itself floating unaware above reality. It loses touch. It is worthless for dealing with current business. It profits nothing in carrying out practical affairs (Heidegger, 1959–1966, p. 46).

Ironically, Heidegger's descriptions of the suspicions of meditative thinking may be one thing agreed upon by nurses in education, especially in college and university settings, and nurses in practice. Calculative thinking is the primary mode of thought used by nursing educators, who apply scientific theory to practice, as well as that of practitioners, who seek new methodologies by drawing on practical experience. Although Heidegger wrote that calculative thinking is "justified and needed in its own way," (p. 46) his major argument was that meditative thinking is also required. Calculative thinking without meditative thinking is blind, because it tells us how to do something but neglects the meaning of what we are doing. But for meditative thinking to disclose meaning, it must be *rooted*. In fact, Heidegger put so much stress on rootedness that his students humorously claimed that he had roots instead of toes. It is calculative thinking that lacks roots, because through theories, it seeks objective knowledge and methods good for anyone, in any place, in any time. In contrast, meditative thinking is rooted in the particular people who dwell in particular places, during particular times. But what would rootedness mean for nursing? Obviously, it would refer to a particular practice which is developed historically during a particular time and in a particular place. Such rooted meditation affirms the worth and integrity of nursing practice by seeking the meaning of nursing as practiced rather than from the perspective of another field outside of nursing. In so doing, nursing is articulated in a way that dissolves the problem of the separation of theory from practice which plagues contemporary nursing.

Since the modern practice of nursing was developed, for the most part, in a hospital setting, we will focus our meditation on nursing practice in that setting, although we recognize that contemporary nursing takes place in a much wider context. Further, we are aware that meditating on nursing as practice opens us to the charge of defending a purely traditional approach to nursing practice. However, Heidegger's contention that meditative thinking must be rooted was hardly traditional, since he believed that rooted meditation not only disclosed actual practice but opened it up for innovative thought which could change practice, not by application of calculative methodology but by recognizing and realizing new possibilities already inherent in practice.

The title of this book suggests that it will both articulate the sense of nursing and develop a philosophy of practice from within the phenomenological tradition. Articulation of the practice of nursing fosters understanding of that practice, while understanding that practice encourages philosophy to become relevant to the lived world. By lived world we mean, with Maurice Merleau-Ponty (1962), that the "world is not what I think, but what I live through" (p. xvi–xvii). Such mutual enrichment of nursing and philosophy, while it is interesting in its own right, should improve the practice of both nursing and philosophy. Stephen Toulmin (1982) points to the beneficial effect on philosophy of actually getting down to cases in his article entitled, "How Medicine Saved the Life of Ethics." While agreeing with Toulmin's contention that getting down to cases has a beneficial effect on ethics, Stanley Hauerwas (1986) points out that Toulmin's assessment is over-optimistic in that "many of the books written in medical ethics look just like standard introductory texts in general ethics"

(p. 3) and that "what is remarkable is that confrontation with medicine has had almost no effect on how philosophers and theologians continue to think about ethics" (p. 4). Hauerwas' contention confirms what Bishop discovered when she first attempted to understand moral issues by applying traditional philosophical approaches to them. Merely applying philosophy to nursing does not necessarily bring about a more adequate understanding of nursing but can have the opposite effect in leading nurses away from nursing practice by forcing thought about nursing into preconceived philosophical molds. Such applied philosophy follows the same prescriptive pattern as natural or behavioral science. Therefore, it is necessary to select a way of practicing philosophy appropriate for articulating the practice of nursing. We have found phenomenological philosophy particularly appropriate, because it brings to consciousness the sense of nursing which is already inherent in practice, rather than imposing meanings on it from outside. Further, this way of philosophizing, by taking seriously the integrity and worth of nursing practice, forces philosophers (and perhaps some academic nurses) to leave the academy and to confront the lived world where they must contend with the ambiguities, problems, and challenges faced by nurses in their actual practice.

We are not contending that types of philosophy other than phenomenology are unable to enhance understanding of nursing practice. Certainly we are not arguing that scholars from outside nursing cannot make important contributions to the understanding of nursing. In fact, the assumptions on which this book is predicated is that philosophers have much to contribute to the understanding of nursing practice. We draw on the insights and interpretations of Hans Georg Gadamer (1976–1981), Alasdair MacIntyre (1984), Stephen Strasser (1985), Edmund Husserl (1911–1965), Martin Heidegger (1959–1966), and others to help us articulate the meaning of nursing. We do, however, contend that the attempt to prescribe health care practice from outside that practice, whether the prescription is done by philosophers, ethicists, natural scientists, or behavioral scientists, distorts practice. Perhaps this is the reason some health care practitioners have become wary of philosophers and ethicists working in health care (Cassell, 1988, pp. vii–ix). Such general condemnations are unfortunate because philosophers and ethicists have made and are making very important contributions to understanding and improving health care by bringing their expertise to bear on health care practice. For example, Eric Cassell (1988) says that Richard Zaner has helped physicians understand that the "profession requires a new understanding of ethics, developed in the light of medicine's special activity—the care of sick persons by physicians" (p. viii). Zaner has immersed himself in medical practice and used his expert understanding of phenomenological philosophy to articulate that practice. The excellent and numerous examples in his articulation of medicine attest to his ability to think from within medical practice. These examples also indicate sound phenomenological analysis. Paul Ricouer (1977) indicated the importance of examples when, in giving the essence of phenomenology for those unfamiliar with it, he stated that phenomenology was concerned with meaning, treated meaning in terms of essence, and gave essence through well-chosen examples. Certainly, other types of philosophy have much to contribute to understanding health care, but phenomenology, by its very nature, begins with and focuses on that which is being considered as it is present in the experience of persons. In the case of nursing, this means beginning with and focusing on nursing practice. Perhaps this is the reason a growing number of interpreters of nursing practice have turned to phenomenology, such as Patricia Benner, Nancy Diekelmann, David Allen, Marilyn Ray, Jean Watson, Anna Omery, Sally Gadow, and many others.

The phenomenological approach to nursing offers one way to lessen the current conflict in nursing between the "hospital traditionalists" and the "academic reformers." The hospital traditionalists tend to defend nursing as it has been articulated and practiced in the past. They usually regard nursing as practical in the narrow sense and favor the education of nursing in hospital programs, as has traditionally been done. They stress practical methodology and leave major decisions concerning overall patient care to physicians and hospital bureaucrats. For some traditionalists in nursing, reform of nursing practice involves tinkering with the methodology rather than improving nursing care within the context of an overall health care system aimed at fostering the physical and psychological well-being of patients.

The opponents of the traditionalist approach in the academy seek to make nursing an intellectual discipline in its own right. To do this, they contend that nursing needs to develop theories which set nursing apart from other health care practices. They favor putting all nursing education in colleges and universities and requiring baccalaureate degrees and even masters degrees for practice. Being in a university setting, they attempt theoretical articulations of nursing as a basis for nursing research.

The attempt to reform nursing from the academy has taken two general directions. The first direction is taken from other professional schools, especially schools of medicine, and tends to stress the development of nursing as a profession and, in alliance with medical science and technology, to treat nursing as an applied science. The second tendency is to seek help from the social and/or behavioral sciences by copying their theories and research procedures in the study of nursing. Those who follow this tendency often regard nursing as an applied social or behavioral science.

These applied science approaches to nursing often involve an implicit degeneration of nursing practice in that they suggest that for nursing to be a discipline worthy of inclusion in a university, it must copy medicine or the behavioral and/or social sciences. When theories are taken from other disciplines and applied to practice, those theories tend to be divorced from actual practice. Since such theories do not develop out of practice, they tend to multiply in direct proportion to the number of theorists. "Everyone has his own theory," so to speak. Thus, when these theories are actually applied to nursing practice, nursing itself loses its sense of unity and integrity.

But nurses need not choose between either making nursing an applied science or maintaining traditional practice with its context determined by others. Fortunately, there is another possibility. It is possible both to affirm the tradition and to recognize that contemporary developments require changes in nursing practice and nursing education. One can regard nursing as an important practice, with a proud tradition, which is in a period of rapid transition due to progress within nursing practice itself and changes in health care practice in general. One needed change that is already occurring is the placement of nursing education within a broader academic setting. Nursing also requires specific theory and research to articulate and improve practice, but such theory and research should start with and come back to nursing practice itself. This does not mean that medical science and technology or theories from the social sciences cannot make a contribution to the practice of nursing. Indeed, as we shall show later through the use of the hermeneutic spiral, both can be incorporated into nursing practice without changing the practice into an applied science. What is needed is theory and research appropriate for nursing as practiced.

Phenomenology and hermeneutics can show how to articulate nursing practice from within. We believe this will become evident as we attempt to articulate nursing practice drawing on that philosophical tradition. Therefore, we will not treat phenomenology and hermeneutics explicitly. We will, however, develop a philosophy of practice from within that tradition that will begin and end with a concrete practice; namely, nursing. We will treat the philosophy of practice generally in chapters 4 and 5 because we believe that examining the nature of practice is essential to understanding the practice of nursing. Our treatment of the philosophy of practice rests on two assumptions. First, attempting to articulate the sense of nursing without philosophical meditation detaches nursing from the lived world which nourishes it and within which it develops. Second, a philosophy of practice, apart from treating concrete practice, is vacuous.

From the philosophical perspective, the investigation of

nursing practice makes philosophy of practice concrete. A philosophy of practice should begin and end by considering actual practice. The current situation in nursing is well-suited for such consideration. There is a growing interest in the philosophy of nursing, especially as interpreted by phenomenological philosophy. Fortunately, this interest has not yet been institutionalized. Thus, philosophy tends to be concerned with actual nursing practice rather than with philosophical treatments of the philosophy of nursing. When a philosophy of practice becomes institutionalized, as for example in philosophy of education, specialists tend to speak to each other rather than to practitioners. In addition, they tend to speak from various schools of philosophy. For example, the philosophy of education was dominated by the pragmatists during the 1930s, 40s and early 50s; since then analytic philosophers have controlled the discipline. When this occurs, the focus is on the implications of a particular type of philosophy for practice rather than on the philosophical articulation and improvement of practice. Then, not only is practice devalued, but so is philosophy. Rather than practicing philosophy, one merely applies a previously worked-out philosophy to the practice at hand. Thus it is appropriately called applied philosophy. In contrast, when one actually philosophizes from within and through practice, it is appropriately called philosophy of practice.

We believe that the philosophy of nursing, when appropriately developed, actually becomes a philosophy of practice. In chapter 2, we will examine four attempts to articulate nursing as a practice. First, we will explore Patricia Benner's (1984) thorough and extensive treatment of nursing practice from a phenomenological perspective. Her study disclosed the unique area of nursing practice which distinguishes it from other health care practices. Some might designate this as nursing's area of autonomy, but we prefer to call it the area in which nurses exercise their legitimate authority, for reasons which will become evident later. In addition, we will articulate the in-between aspect of nursing practice drawing on Tristram Engelhardt (1982, 1985), Timothy Sheard (1980) and Sally Gadow (1980, 1982, 1985).

By in-between we mean that, in addition to exercising legitimate authority, nurses practice in between physicians, patients, and hospital bureaucrats in a unique way.

Nursing practice is situated within health care practice and thus must be considered as a practice related to other health care practices. In chapter 3 we explore the health care context within which nurses practice. Drawing on Edmund Pellegrino (1982, 1985) and others (Kestenbaum, 1982), we will argue that all of health care, including medicine, is concerned primarily with caring for the ill, and thus is a human endeavor. However, this endeavor must incorporate medical science and technology aimed at cure. The spectacular advances in ability to cure have tempted some to regard health care practice as applied science. But we will show that such progress merely makes health care more effective rather than changing its basic nature, which is caring for the ill. Further, we will contend that the primary sense of health care is not scientific or technological but moral.

If health care is primarily a human venture with a moral purpose, it follows that health care practice should be studied by the human sciences rather than the natural or behavioral sciences. In the case of nursing, we will show in chapter 4 that the primary sense of nursing is disclosed by practical human sciences. In developing this theme, we will draw on Stephen Strasser's (1985) distinction between practical science and applied science and between theoretical and practical human sciences. Also Strasser's interpretation of the hermeneutic spiral will show how medical science and technology and theories from the social sciences can be incorporated into nursing practice without making it an applied science. Further, we will show that those investigating such human practices as nursing should share the moral imperative of nursing to foster the physical and psychological well-being of patients regardless of whether their initial interest begins from inside or outside nursing.

An adequate treatment of practice through the human sciences requires a philosophical treatment of practice. In chapter 5 we will develop a philosophy of practice drawing on Gadamer (1976–1981) using examples taken from nursing practice. We will use MacIntyre's (1984) philosophy of virtue to show how practice is related to virtue in nursing. Of special significance to nursing practice are Gadamer's and MacIntyre's interpretation of practice as dynamic. For them a practice is dead when it does not strive to recognize and realize possibilities which are inherent in it. Further, these possibilities give rise to innovations, not only in the way in which nursing is practiced but also in the virtues and aims which give nursing vision and direction.

In chapter 6 we will show that the moral sense of nursing practice is the dominant sense of nursing as actually practiced. However, this dominant sense is often not explicitly articulated by nurses when describing their own practice. In a study of fulfillment in nursing, we found that the dominant sense of nursing was moral and personal rather than professional and technical. Further, nurses felt most fulfilled when professional and technical competency was incorporated in nursing practice which realized its moral sense within a personal relationship.

In chapter 7 we will show that the moral sense of nursing requires a new approach to nursing ethics. In this approach moral issues and problems are inherent within nursing practice itself rather than being the result of advances in medical science and technology as many philosophical ethicists claim. When traditional philosophical ethics is applied to nursing, it emphasizes individual and professional autonomy to the neglect of trust and mutuality. We will show that, in practice, nursing ethics is based primarily on trust and mutuality. This implies that the in-between situation of nurses, which is such a thorn in the side of those who stress autonomy, is actually a privileged position from which to make moral decisions concerning patient care.

The last chapter will focus on the personal side of nursing implied by the moral sense of nursing practice. Nursing is primarily a personal relationship between nurse and patient which fosters the well-being of the patient. The personal aspect of nursing practice has three senses. The first

sense means that nurses must practice nursing in a way that
expresses their particular way of being in relationship to patients. Second, personal means that patients are to be regarded as persons with dignity and respect even when being
treated impersonally. Finally, personal means that nurses
must be open to particular persons as they are encountered
in nursing practice. Personal relationships in nursing practice are developed through communication by speaking and
touching. This requires nurses to communicate, not merely
in the propositional language in which nursing practice is
usually articulated, but also in expressive and evocative language as well. Further, all three modes of language should
be incorporated into an integral language appropriate to the
patient situation and the relationship between nurse and patient.

Since our book is an articulation of nursing from
within practice itself, it should speak forcefully to those
nurses who have a deep appreciation for the caring tradition,
and therefore, find unacceptable the radical approach which
would make nursing either an applied natural or an applied
social science. Also, since it offers a dynamic interpretation
of that tradition which opens new possibilities for innova-
tion from within practice, it should give direction to those
nurses who find a narrow traditionalist approach to nursing
stultifying and out of step with the advances now taking
place in nursing.

Can we actually achieve our goal of articulating *the* essence of nursing from within nursing practice? Although
that is our goal, we are merely fallible beings in time. One
source of our fallibility at this time is that so little has been
done in the philosophy of nursing. For this reason, we hope
that our venture into this neglected area of nursing not only
will help nurses and scholars in nursing to better grasp the
meaning of nursing practice but also will encourage others
to join us in exploring the meaning of nursing philosophically.

Chapter 2

The Practical Sense of Nursing

The practical sense of nursing is an articulation of the essence of the way in which nursing is practiced. Unfortunately, many people think of practical as methods or techniques used in practice. But methods and techniques, isolated from the systems of meaning which give direction to their use in achieving the goods at which they aim, make little sense and hence are not practical at all. Therefore, the practical sense of nursing requires an articulation of the systems of meaning which gives nursing its essential sense. There have been at least four attempts at articulation of the essence of nursing practice: Benner's (1984) extensive study of nursing competencies; Sheard's (1980) comparison of the work worlds of the physician with that of the nurse; Engelhardt's (1985) description of the in-between situation of nurses; and Gadow's (1980) contention that the nature of nursing practice places the nurse in the role of existential advocate for the patient.

Benner's (1984) study of nursing competencies is by far the most extensive and thorough articulation of nursing practice. In fact, Myrtle Aydelotte (1984) has called it a "major contribution to nursing" (p. v). Benner pioneers by offering a phenomenological explication of "the knowledge embedded in actual practice—i.e., that knowledge that accrues over time" (p. 1). She laments the over-reliance on the "sociological perspective" in research which focuses on "role relationships, socialization and acculturation in nursing practice" (p. 1). She believes that nurses have not

13

examined the knowledge embedded in actual nursing practice because they have not understood the difference between practical and theoretical knowledge. She contends that "what's missing are systematic observations of what nurse clinicians learn from their clinical practice" (p. 1).

Benner explored this missing ingredient in nursing research. She and her team contacted over 1,200 nurses through questionnaires and interviews (p. xxv). Using interviews and observations of actual practice of over one hundred nurses, she formulated an understanding of the movement from novice to expert nurse clinician and identified the domains and competencies of nursing practice. By examining patient care episodes given in narrative form by practicing nurses, Benner found thirty-one competencies, which were subsequently classified into seven domains on the "basis of similarity of function and content" (p. 44).

We are less interested in her description of the movement from novice to expert than in that of the domains and competencies. We believe the latter to be a very promising start toward identifying the essence of nursing from actual practice. This, of course, is a fundamental phenomenological move. The movement from novice to expert is not without phenomenological interest, but the nature of our book gives priority to the essence of nursing over how one achieves excellence in nursing practice. However, Benner's description of this movement does indicate that the essence of nursing has to be stated dynamically rather than statically.

Benner, herself, is primarily interested in the knowledge of nursing that comes from practice rather than describing the essence of nursing. But to us, she seems to be setting forth an important preliminary treatment of the essence of nursing. We say preliminary not to depreciate this excellent study, but to show that her book, like ours, is an attempt to begin thinking about nursing in a new way. From her thought-provoking beginning we will develop our own description of the "in-between" sense of nursing and of the moral and personal sense of nursing. We will treat these senses of nursing later in the book, but for now, we will set forth Benner's treatment of a major aspect of the essence of nursing.

In describing the domains and competencies of nursing, Benner is in accord with Ricoeur's (1977) contention that essence is given through well-chosen examples. Benner describes the domains and competencies by giving concrete exemplars in the form of descriptions selected from the interviews in her study rather than by generalized descriptive statements.

There is no generalized treatment of the essence of each of the seven domains of nursing practice. Instead, Benner gives the essence of each of the domains as competencies. These competencies are exemplified from the description of practice in actual situations contributed by the participants in her study. These examples are followed by a summary statement which helps interpret their meaning. We will list each domain and then list the competencies of one domain and give one example and include the summary following the example. Our purpose is not to give a summary of Benner's work but to illustrate what a description of the essence of nursing taken from practice is like. Benner's seven domains of nursing practice are:

(1) the helping role; (2) the teaching-coaching function; (3) the diagnostic and patient-monitoring function; (4) effective management of rapidly changing situations; (5) administering and monitoring therapeutic interventions and regimens; (6) monitoring and ensuring the quality of health care practices; (7) organization and work-role competencies (Benner, 1984, p. 46).

We have selected the domain of the diagnostic and patient-monitoring function because it will not only illustrate the content and examples of one of the domains, but it will also show one of the themes of Benner's work. Benner claims that practice actually contributes to our knowledge of health care. This would mean that nursing practice, itself, provides new knowledge which is used in health care. The area of diagnostic and patient monitoring has developed rapidly in nursing over the past twenty years. Since nurses are the ones who actually are with patients monitoring them during hospitalization, they are in the position to observe changes, especially subtle ones which warn of impending crisis. The competencies Benner lists in this domain are:

(1) detection and documentation of significant changes in a patient's condition; (2) providing an early warning signal: anticipating breakdown and deterioration prior to explicit confirming diagnostic signs; (3) anticipating problems: future think; (4) understanding the particular demands and experiences of an illness; anticipating patient care needs; (5) assessing the patient's potential for wellness and responding to various treatment strategies (Benner, 1984, p. 97).

To illustrate Benner's use of exemplars, we selected the following example of the competency, providing an early warning signal: anticipating breakdown and deterioration prior to explicit confirming diagnostic signs.

Expert Nurse: "We had a patient who had an esophageal dilatation in X-Ray. She was a very uncomplaining woman of about 60 years of age. When she came back her vital signs were OK, and she was up in the bathroom. Later she started getting nauseated and she had streaks of very light pink drainage which I could account for by dilatation procedures, but I just had this feeling that something else was going on. She became worse; she became very nauseated. I called the house officer. Her vital signs were still stable, but I indicated that I wanted the house officer to check her. The house officer examined her but was not ordering any tests. I wanted to order blood work. I pointed out that the patient's nail beds were cyanotic. The house officer was unimpressed. It was almost time for me to go off duty when the patient started having chills with a temperature, so I called the house officer again and said there was something going on with this patient, and that I wanted to see something done for her before I went off duty. Later I found that the patient had a rupture in her esophagus; she also had aspiration pneumonia. Her pulse had gone up

to 150. The house officer credited my persistence in getting early treatment in making a difference in the patient's outcome" (Benner, pp. 100–101).

It is interesting that in the above example that the nurse recognized the early warning signs but the physician did not,
and only the nurse's stubborn persistence led to an examination which prevented disaster. Usually, however, preventing
disaster requires the cooperation of the physician as the following summary statement indicates:

> There are a number of similar examples of early detec-
> tion of a change in patient status before the presence of
> objective, measurable signs. This advanced recognitional
> ability frequently makes a critical difference in patient
> recovery. The effectiveness of this competency, however,
> gets linked with the nurse's skill in getting an appro-
> priate and timely response from the physician (Benner,
> 1984, p. 102).

This summary statement implies that one of the competencies that nurses need is skill in getting cooperation
from physicians. Benner includes this competency in the
domain of monitoring and ensuring the quality of health
care practices. We will later show that this competency is
inherent in the in-between stance of nursing, which is an
essential aspect of nursing practice in the institutional setting. As nurses have increasingly developed their competencies and expanded their legitimate authority, a greater recognition and appreciation by nurses of being in-between may
assist them in seeing the importance of their strategic place
rather than being "visibly uncomfortable talking about this
aspect of their role" (Benner, p. 135).

Some interpreters of nursing, unlike Benner, concen-
trate so exclusively on the need for nurses to develop their
autonomy that they obscure this in-between element of
nursing practice. We will show later that being in-between
places the nurse in a unique position in making moral decision in health care, and we will argue that this unique position is a privileged one.

The Different Work Worlds of Physician and Nurse

For most nurses it will seem odd that their in-between situation is a privileged one for reasons which Sheard (1980) makes evident in his contrast of the work worlds of physicians and nurses. His description of the different structuring of the work of the physician and the nurse in terms of the sense of time, sense of resources, unit of analysis, work assignments, reward, and sense of mastery clearly indicates why nurses might wish to abandon their in-between situation for a more autonomous one. Although recent advances in the self-direction of nurses may make his contrast seem too sharply drawn, the differences he describes still seem, in the main, to be sound. Therefore, we will summarize his contrasts as he describes them.

Generally a physician's time is lived time in that it is structured by a caring relationship with a patient. The way in which this time is lived is determined by the course of the disease, the nature of the treatment, and his relationship to the patient, not by the clock. Generally, a nurse practices by clock time. There are eight to twelve hour schedules, divided by tasks to be performed at given times in sequential order. Often conflicts between physicians and nurses result from this different sense of time. The physician "owns his time" and usually a portion of the nurse's time. He allots the nurse's time by giving orders which require the use of the nurse's time. The nurse's time is also allotted by a hospital schedule with definite and routine requirements to be done according to the clock.

Generally, physicians have a sense of abundant resources. Usually what they order is delivered by others and paid for by health insurance. The nurse, in contrast, generally has to secure what the physician wants from hospital administration, which is concerned with balancing the budget. In addition, the nurse who spends much more time with the patient than the physician must face the patient's concern over mounting bills, all of which may not be paid by insurance.

Physicians and nurses experience their relationship

with the patient differently. Generally, the physician's relationship to the patient occurs over time as determined by the care required for a particular patient. In contrast, nurses generally have their relationship to the patient structured by hospital and physician requirements arranged in clock time. They rarely work with the patient over the entire course of the patient's illness. This, of course, means that the work assignment of the nurse is determined by others and ordered in ways which suit their needs. Often, they are caught between the hospital's need for efficiency to reduce costs and the physician's demands on their time. In contrast, physicians generally arrange their own work schedule with certain constraints such as availability of operating rooms, X-rays, and laboratory tests.

The type and size of rewards are very different for physician and nurse. Nurses by and large work for an hourly or a fixed wage. Therefore, their financial rewards bear little relationship to the effort, concern and ingenuity they put into their work. The nurse's wage is determined by hospital administration and how well the nurse performs her functions, according to the hospital's standards—not according to the patient's evaluation. In contract, physicians generally are paid on the basis of fee for service; therefore, there is a direct relationship between their effort and amount of work and the reward received.

Physicians have a strong sense of mastery over their work. If to live according to your own projects is living authentically, physicians live authentically for the most part. They decide the patients for whom they will care; they structure that care; they decide the fee to be charged; and they determine how much time and effort to put into each case, within limits. Nurses have much less mastery over their work. Their time is scheduled by others and their tasks and relationships to patients are in large part dictated by hospital policy, routines, and physician demands. Shifting assignments may inhibit the development of therapeutic and personal relationships with patients.

Sheard's analysis may be too sharply drawn to show the changes in physician-nurse relationships which have resulted from increases in legitimate authority in contemporary nursing. However, it does clearly indicate that a nurse's work world is very different from that of the physician in that the nurse must work in-between the physician, hospital bureaucrat, and patient in a way that is different in kind, rather than merely in degree, from the physician. We will examine this further by following Engelhardt's description of the "in-between" situation in which nurses are caught.

In-between Situation of Nurses

Engeldhardt (1985) has designated nurses as the "people in-between," because "nurses give their care under the scrutiny of two rather powerful individuals: the patient and the physician" (p. 71). The physician's power comes from his authority in health care matters which results both from his greater knowledge and technical skill in medicine and from the legal right "to prescribe drugs and perform essential lifesaving and pain-reducing procedures" (p. 72). The patients have the right to decide what they will allow to be done to them. A growing number of court decisions including *Nathanson v. Kline, Canterbury v. Spence,* and in *Re: President and Directors of Georgetown College,* all clearly recognize the patient as a source of authority for health care (Engelhardt, 1985). Thus, although patients are often disabled by disease or are ignorant concerning their condition and prognosis, they "join as co-equals with physicians in authorizing therapeutic endeavors" (Engelhardt, 1985, pp. 72–73).

On the other hand, the authority and rights of the nurse are ambiguous. "Nurses are caught between physicians, on the one hand, who are authorities regarding scientific and technological knowledge, and are *in authority,* and patients on the other hand, who give authority for health care endeavors" (Engelhardt, 1985, p. 73). The result of this in-between moral and legal situation is clearly evident in the famous *Tuma v. Board of Nursing of State of Idaho* (1979) case in which the nurse was caught in-between the patient's request for information and the physician's established authority. Engelhardt asks, "Did Tuma need the authority of a physician to offer therapeutic alternatives, or is it sufficient that she is authorized by the patient?" (p. 73). He further contends that since the nurse is "treated as an agent of both, the conflict can be deep and intractable" (p. 73). Thus, in the Tuma case, "the Court recognized the unclarity regarding what would or would not count as unprofessional conduct, and in doing so acknowledged the ambiguity of the position of nurses" (p. 73). Obviously, for Engelhardt, the in-between situation of nurses refers to the ambiguous situation in which they are caught rather than a privileged position from which to foster communal decisions concerning health care as we will attempt to show later.

While Engelhardt clearly shows why the nurse is caught in-between the patient's rights and the physician's authority, he neglects, in his treatment of the in-between, the growing power of the hospital as an institution, increasingly controlled by bureaucrats. Mila Aroskar (1985) indicates that the hospital bureaucracy constitutes a third force which nurses must consider in making decisions. She calls this the marketing view of the hospital and contrasts it with interpretations which contend that hospitals should serve physicians and/or patients. The marketing approach is clearly evident in proprietary hospitals, but it is implicit in the struggle for non-profit hospitals to survive with present-day high costs and prospective reimbursement. Both factors combine to limit the length of hospital stay and to encourage the hospital to curtail costs. This often requires curtailing services. One costly service in any hospital is provided by the nursing staff. When hospitals have decreased their nursing staffs and created an oversupply of nurses, which has happened frequently, the consequence in a market situation is that nurses have less power. In contrast, physicians bring patients to the hospital and the patients are the customers who pay. The nurse is caught in-between the physician, the paying customer and the hospital bureaucrats charged with keeping the hospital in the black.

The old adage, "Physician's admit patient to the hospital; nurses don't," neglects the fact that nurses provide much of the care for which patients require hospitalization. After all, they provide the twenty-four-hour care that most patients require. Thus, the cost of that care depends on the acuity level of the patient. Patients do pay for nursing services just as they pay for physician's services and the services of the radiologist and the medical technologist. However, charges for the services of the physician, radiologist and medical technologist are billed or itemized separately, while charges for the nurses' services generally are not. When nursing services are charged to the patient, like the services of the laboratory, the operating room and the radiology departments, it calls attention to the fact that patients require hospitalization because they need *nursing care*, not expensive, Spartan board and room. When hospital bureaucrats do not recognize that nursing care is an essential ingredient in hospital care, they are apt to reduce expenses by cutting nursing staff. Even those who recognize the need for adequate nursing care find it easier to cut nursing staff than to deny the requests of physicians for new and expensive equipment. Physicians do, after all, admit patients to the hospital; nurses do not. But physicians do bring demands for supplies and services which nurses are usually expected to secure, often under pressure from administration to contain costs; thus, they are caught in-between the physician and the hospital bureaucrat.

Nursing as Existential Advocacy

Sally Gadow's (1980) existential phenomenological description of the nurse as an existential advocate could lead nurses to understand their in-between situation as a privileged one rather than an unfortunate one in which they are trapped. To do this, Gadow would need to relate existential advocacy to traditional nursing. Instead she attempts to develop "a new philosophy that sets contemporary nursing distinctively apart from both traditional nursing and modern medicine" (p. 79). She contends that "nursing ought to be defined philosophically rather than sociologically, that is defined by the ideal nature and purpose of the nurse-patient relation rather than by a specific set of behaviors" (p. 80). She certainly does show how existential phenomenology can enhance one's understanding of nursing, regardless of the soundness of her claim that "existential advocacy" is "*the* essence of nursing" (p. 81).

She describes existential advocacy in three ways:

1. the nurse's assistance to individuals in exercising their right of self-determination, through decisions which express the full and unique complexity of their values.

2. a mode of involvement with patients which necessarily engages the entire self of the nurse.

3. assistance to patients in unifying the experience of the lived body and the object body at a level that incorporates and transcends both (Gadow, 1980, p. 97).

Her first description of existential advocacy is "based upon the principles that freedom of self-determination is the most fundamental and valuable human right" (p. 84). She regards this right as so important that it "ought not to be infringed upon even in the interest of health" (p. 84). Although this implies that those in health care should not base decisions on what they believe patients "*should want,*" it does not focus on "protecting the individual's right to do what they want to do." Instead it affirms that patients ought to be "*assisted* by nursing to *authentically* exercise their freedom of determination."

> It is the effort to help persons *become clear about what they want* to do, by helping them discern and clarify their values in the situation and on the basis of that self-examination, to reach decisions which express their reaffirmed, perhaps recreated, complex of values (p. 85).

Her second description of existential advocacy concerns the personal versus the professional in nursing. She rightly objects to the common contention that the personal is inner and subjective and that the professional is outer and objective. The differences between the nurse and the patient concern how they deal with "illness as a personal experience" (p. 87). The patient is focused on her illness and how it affects her life; she intensely experiences her pain and suffering. The professional, on the other hand, is focused on the patient, her distress and symptoms, and how she can be of help to the patient.

The third description concerns the distinction between the lived body and the body object. To make this distinction clear, she uses as an example a gynecological examination.

> For the patient, the part of the body being examined is often an extremely personal part of the self, perhaps the most private and emotionally invested part of the body. In the clinical situation, "the pelvic area is like any other part of the body," i.e., the individual examining the patient is "working on a technical object and not a person" (p. 93).

Her contention is certainly not that the patient is focused on the lived body and the nurse on the body object. Instead she contends that the nurse should attend to the patient's lived body, which is experienced immediately by the patient as pain, debilitation or incapacity. The nurse, by drawing on her knowledge of the body object, can help the patient understand one meaning of what is happening to her lived body. This makes it possible for the patient "to establish a conscious identification with aspects of his being which were previously undifferentiated, but have, through illness and objectivity, made themselves known" (p. 96). The nurse "affirms the value of the lived body through the intimacy of physical care and comforting" and "the reality of the body object by interpreting to the patients their experience in terms of an objective framework—usually science" (p. 96). As existential advocate she helps the patient unify the lived body and the body object in a way that brings about "a conscious unifying of self and body" (p. 96).

Gadow summarizes "advocacy nursing as the participation with the patient in determining the *personal meaning* which the experience of illness, suffering, or dying is to have for that individual" (p. 97). She contends that the person uniquely qualified to be an existential advocate is the nurse.

A glaring omission from Gadow's reason for a nurse's being an existential advocate is an examination of those competencies which nurses learn from engaging in a practice, like those described by Benner, through which the nurses give care to the patient. Perhaps the reason for this omission is her emphasis on the need for nurses to help patients understand the meaning of their experience of illness to the neglect of how nursing care helps alleviate or extricate them from their situation. In short, she neglects what she rejects; namely, traditional practice with its competencies enmeshed in that system of meaning called nursing care.

She also misses the significance of another practical sense of traditional nursing care; namely, the in-between situation of the nurse. We will contend that this in-between situation is one reason why nurses would make excellent existential advocates. This will become evident through questioning the feasibility of existential advocacy as the mandated essence of nursing. Should patients not be able to choose their own existential advocate? If so, they might choose any member of the health care team who is close to them or someone other than the health care team, such as a family member or a friend. After all, the choice of an existential advocate is primarily a personal one. The person with whom the patient is most closely related and trusts most completely, however, may not be the best choice as an existential advocate in the health care situation, as Gadow points out. A close friend or relative probably would not have the understanding, skill, and power to be the advocate for a patient in a health care setting that a nurse has. For this reason, the nurse is in a unique position to be an existential advocate *because* of her in-between position. She understands the medical perspective, the hospital policies and procedures, and she often has a close relationship with the patient. This situation not only makes her an ideal patient advocate, but also an advocate of the physician's advice and hospital policy when patients fail to understand how either fosters their well-being. Nurses usually more than any other member of the health care team are best suited for this kind of advocacy because they work from the in-between situation.

Existential advocacy refers more to the personal and moral sense of nursing than to the practical sense and, as we shall show later, is an important ingredient in these essential senses of nursing. But is existential advocacy *the* essence of nursing, as Gadow contends, or even an essential aspect of nursing comparable to the nurse's exercising legitimate authority, as described in Benner's competencies, and the nurse's acting from an in-between situation? It is obvious that both of the foregoing are essential ingredients in nursing. It seems inconceivable that one could be a competent nurse without practicing the competencies articulated by Benner. Also, in most settings, it seems inconceivable that one could be a competent nurse without being able to work in-between the physician, hospital or other bureaucrats, and patient.

Could one be a competent or excellent nurse without being an existential advocate? Certainly, an excellent nurse should be willing to be a patient's existential advocate and, as we have indicated, is usually best suited for such advocacy. There is no doubt that a nurse should be an existential advocate when that advocacy is clearly related to illness and the full recovery from illness. But "determining the personal meaning which the experience of illness, suffering and dying is to have for the individual" involves the nurse in discussing the meaning of another's life, albeit, in relation to illness, suffering and death. Certainly one could question whether being a nurse requires or entitles one to such intimate and personal involvement in another's life unless invited to be by the other person. Few persons would want another person to become intimately involved in their lives merely on the grounds that they had been assigned to them as their nurse. A nurse-patient relationship legitimizes specific kinds of care which often involve the meaning of one's life. But pursuing that involvement beyond the care given should be by invitation only. Certainly deciding about entering such personal relationships is a right as important as self-direction. In matters which go beyond specific health care, advocacy concerns the general moral imperative which requires persons to care for other persons when they need and are *willing* to receive such care. We are raising the issue not to separate the moral and personal from the professional; we agree with Gadow that such a separation is unwarranted. Instead, we are attempting to lay the groundwork for our contention that nursing is essentially a moral enterprise involving personal relationships with patients. Further, we will contend later that the moral and personal are an inherent and essential aspect of nursing. Existential advocacy is an important aspect of the moral and personal essence of nursing. But before one can treat existential advocacy as essential to nursing, one must show that the moral and personal are essential and integral in nursing practice. We will attempt to show this in health care, in general, in the next chapter and in nursing specifically later in the book. For now, we merely claim that essential ingredients in the essence of nursing are excellent practice as described by Benner and acting from the in-between situation described by Engelhardt and others.

Chapter 3

The Human Sense of Health Care

Nurses must not only work cooperatively with others in health care from their unique in-between situation, but nursing itself must be understood from within the context of an articulation of health care practice. In this chapter we will argue that health care practice should be understood primarily as a human enterprise concerned with the caring relationship between physicians and nurses and ill persons. Understanding this caring relationship requires articulation of the human meaning of both illness and health care practice. The alternative to the caring approach to health care is the curing approach, which regards health care as technology, the sense of which comes from the applied science called medical science.

The primary issue is not, however, the purpose of health care, whether cure or care, but the way in which practice, itself, comes about and is carried out. Certainly, traditional health care practice evolved over time out of medical and nursing experience rather than through application of

This chapter includes material from "The Moral Sense and Health Care" by Scudder and Bishop, in *The Moral Sense in the Communal Significance of Life, Analecta Husserliana 20* [edited by] A-T. Tymieniecka, pp. 125–158, copyright 1986 by D. Reidel Publishing Co. Used by permission.

Excerpts from "The Foundation of Health Care: Natural or Human" by Scudder and Bishop, copyright 1985 by *The Humanistic Psychologist*. Used by permission.

scientific discoveries to medical practice. Even medicine, which has often wrapped itself in a mantle of scientific cure, actually has been primarily concerned with caring for ill patients. As Pellegrino (1985) points out, cure in the sense of "the eradication of the cause of an illness or disease—to the radical interruption and reversal, of the natural history of a disorder" (p. 9) has, with a few exceptions, only been a possibility for physicians who entered the profession following World War II. The spectacular successes in the ability to cure, especially since World War II, according to Pellegrino, have inclined many physicians to think of medical practice as curing through scientific means and understanding rather than as the traditional practice of caring for ill patients (Pellegrino, 1985, p. 9).

Before World War II, physicians were more engaged in healing than in curing. By healing we mean simply that physicians were able to enhance the functioning of the healing powers of the body. For Florence Nightingale, nursing was like medicine in that both merely fostered healing. This conception of health care so dominated her thought that she actually opposed the theory of germs and contagion which eventually made it possible for physicians to cure some disease (Rosenberg, 1979). Although cure is now possible in some cases, much of medical practice still concerns healing. Doubtless, in the future, with the advance of medical science, cure in the radical sense will become increasingly a function of medicine. As this occurs, cure has the possibility of becoming the foundation of medical practice.

> But the golden era of specific therapy has just begun, and its promises are still to be fully apprehended. We are now in the era of synthesis of natural and man-made agents, designed to attack the molecular and cellular sources of disease. We can invade any body cavity to excise, reconstruct, or transplant disease organs and tissues. Radical cure and restoration—not amelioration or disease containment—have become realistic and legitimate goals of medicine (Pellegrino, 1985, pp. 9–10).

This radical transformation of medicine realistically raises, for the first time, the issue of whether medicine is concerned with cure rather than care.

If medicine is primarily founded on cure, then the foundations of medicine are the medical sciences which make cure possible. Medicine itself becomes a technology derived from medical science. The relationship between medical science and practice would be analogous to the relationship of physics to mechanical technology or chemistry to chemical engineering. Thus, medicine itself would be an applied science drawing from various sciences, especially biochemistry, and medical "practice" would be a technology derived from medical science. Critics of this position could and have argued that medical science is not yet perfected enough for most medical practice to be based on it. However, in principle this would still mean that medical practice ought to be derived from medical science when possible. That is, as medical science advances, the old-fashioned and archaic view of medical practice as caring should be replaced by curing.

If medical practice is founded on cure and cure is founded on medical science and physicians become technicians, what would nurses become, especially since they have identified their profession with caring? Presumably, if health care becomes cure, nurses would become general assistants to physicians in effecting cure. Of course, they also would comfort and render aid to patients as they have done traditionally. But if they insist that nursing is essentially care in the direct sense, then medical technicians would gradually replace them, both in number and importance, unless they joined those health care professionals with the technical and specialized knowledge necessary to support curing. But then they would be nurses in name only. Nightingale understood this at the inception of the nursing profession when she argued that the theories of germs and contagion would lead to a conception of medicine which would diminish the importance of nursing as a practice in its own right (Rosenberg, 1979).

If cure founded on medical science is the basis of health

care, then medical ethics becomes bioethics. Indeed, bioethics is what medical ethics is often called. Although
many health care professionals and non-professionals use
the term in a vague way to mean medical ethics in general,
the foundation of bioethics is clear in the way moral issues
are treated. The ability of medical technology to prolong life
creates the problem of euthanasia; advances in obstetrics
and neonatology create the "right to life" issues; artificial
organs and transplants create the problem of who should receive scarce items and how money should be distributed in
health care. The assumption underlying these problems and
many more is that advances in medical science create problems in medical ethics which have previously not been
faced. For this reason, philosophers, theologians, and other
ethicists are said to be needed to work with medical personnel on resolving these problems.

In contrast to the bioethical assumption that moral
problems result from advances in medical science, the caring approach to health care assumes that health care practice itself is a moral enterprise. The primary goal of all
health care is to promote the physical and psychological
well-being of persons. Moral problems are not primarily the
result of advances in medical science but are inherent in the
relationship of physician, nurse and patient. Therefore, the
moral problems of medical care are not the result of advances in medical science but have been in existence as long
as there have been healers and the ill. This, of course, means
that moral problems are not "caused" by advances in medical science and technology but are inherent in the practice
of medicine itself. Medical practice, according to Pellegrino
(1982), "is a special moral enterprise because it is grounded
in a special personal relationship between one who is ill and
another who professes to heal." Therefore, "healing is a
mutual act that aims to repair the defects created by the experience of illness" (p. 157).

Obviously, the foundation of the caring approach to
health care is a moral relationship between physician, nurse
and patient as the term "health care" implies. This relationship begins with an illness (Kestenbaum, 1982) which

brings the person to the physician. Thus, the physician patient relationship is initiated by the illness experienced by the patient rather than by the disease diagnosed by the physician. Illness concerns a disruption in the lived world of the person, not a pathological description of disease. As Engelhardt (1982) points out, illness is what is experienced by the person who becomes a patient while disease is the pathological definition of that illness used in diagnosis by a physician. Disease, as Benner (1989) points out, refers to a taxonomy which designates the "manifestation of aberration at the cellular, tissue or organ level" (p. 8) rather than the lived experience of illness.

In everyday life people often confuse the meanings of illness and disease. For example, when a husband was asked about his wife's illness, he replied that he did not know what it was. In fact, he had had the same illness a few days prior and knew well what she was experiencing. What he did not know was the pathological category to which it belonged. Also, he believed that the illness was of short duration and did not require medical attention. He was sure that medical attention was not required because in his case, the body had healed itself in a short time without medical treatment. Much illness is still handled without professional help and often with folk medicine.

When the disruption by illness is severe enough that a person needs assistance, the person seeks medical help and becomes a patient. Both illness and being a patient are human experiences which have been well described phenomenologically. Illness ruptures our relationship to the world, according to Gadow (1982):

> The immediacy of that being-in-the-world is ruptured by incapacity, the experience of being unable to act as desired or to escape being acted upon in ways that are not desired. Immediacy, in short, is shattered by constraint (p. 88).

Mary Rawlinson (1982) describes illness as a rupture in the man-world relationship focusing on the lived body.

Illness names that experience in which our own everyday embodied capacities fail us. Illness obstructs our ordinary access to the world and presents the body as a signifier for the way in which we are limited and can be impeded in our encounter with the world (p. 74).

She contends that illness alters this relationship in four ways. First, our body becomes the center of our concerns. Usually we are not aware of our bodies.

When our embodiment fails, we discover that embodiment ordinarily means reaching for, going toward, attending to what is present, and in short, enjoying the capacity to encounter what is other (Rawlinson, 1982, p. 75).

When we become ill—almost in direct proportion to the severity of our illness—the body fills our consciousness.

Whereas our embodied capacities ordinarily provide the background to the figure of our worldly involvements, in illness our body, and particularly that aspect which pains, becomes itself the figure of our intention against which all else is merely background (Rawlinson, 1982, p. 75).

Second, illness "confounds our capacity to expect. Our embodiment seems unreliable and unpredictable" (p.75). This unreliability ranges from temporary disruptions in our everyday activities, to adjusting to a permanent loss of some capacity, to the termination of all possibilities in the near future. Third, illness makes us aware that our concerns are not merely determined by our own choosing. The ill person does not decide to become absorbed with illness and pain. This imposition brings an acute awareness of our own finiteness and of the possible and actual loss of self. And finally, "illness distorts our ordinary relationship with others insofar as it debilitates, humiliates, and isolates" (Rawlinson, 1982, pp. 75–76). Illness isolates us from others because of our absorption with our own illness and suffering and because others tend to think of the ill as not like me. In addition, illness

> results in a surrender of one's autonomy and integrity of person out of necessity or in hope that this surrender will be in the end useful in the effort to recover those capacities which the illness obstructs and threatens. This surrender makes one vulnerable and leaves one at the mercy of others in significant ways (Rawlinson, 1982, p. 77).

In summary, Rawlinson (1982) states why we disvalue illness:

> (1) the obstruction of our capacity to 'possibilize' and take up involvements in the world, (2) the way in which illness disrupts and derails our direction of our own histories, (3) the extraordinary dependence and lack of self-sufficiency and self-control which illness brings (p. 78).

People become patients when illness leads them to seek professional help. As Pellegrino (1985) points out, we experience "a pain in the chest, the finding of a lump, the loss of appetite, morning nausea, dizziness on bending over . . . which leads us to seek help" (p. 14). According to Pellegrino, seeking professional help is the first element in the patient-physician relationship. The act of profession is the second element in the patient-physician relationship. When the physician accepts the patient, he or she makes two implicit promises, according to Pellegrino. First, the physician is competent and possesses the knowledge which one needs. Second, he or she promises to use that knowledge in the patient's interest. This relationship is therefore based on profession and trust. Thus, it is different from a commercial relationship which is based on mutual self-interest or a legal relationship which is based on contract.

An ill patient becomes extremely vulnerable when he entrusts his life to a physician's professional care. The gap between patient vulnerability and professional knowledge and skill is closed during the act of medicine. This is the third element in the physician-patient relationship, in which the physician and patient come to a decision about what to do about the illness—a decision which is technically right and morally good.

> Medical science can determine what is physically wrong, what can be done about it and what is likely to be the outcome. But it cannot tell what ought to be done for the good of a particular patient. If you follow that cure model, the biomedical model, then what is medically good, what is medically indicated, what is scientifically correct becomes what is good for the patient. But reflect for a moment and you'll see the two are not the same. The good decision must also fit this particular person's concept of the good life and of the way he or she wants to live (Pellegrino, 1985, pp. 15–16).

Since medical decisions aim ultimately at the good of a particular patient, medical practice cannot be determined or founded primarily on natural science, even though that natural science plays a significant role in medicine. Nor can an adequate description of medical practice be taken from medical science. Note that Pellegrino's phenomenological description of the physician-patient relationship is not drawn from medical science but from the articulation of the essence of medical practice. The essence is a caring relationship which begins when illness brings a person to the physician. Illness signifies the experience of limitation or debilitation which prevents the person from living as he is accustomed to live or wants to live. Ill persons become patients when they seek the help of the physician and the physician agrees to give that help. This agreement is a commitment on the part of the physician to use his skill and knowledge to promote the physical and psychological well-being of the patient in accord with the patient's view of the good life. Thus, the medical relationship is founded on an implicit moral commitment embodied in medical practice itself.

The study of medicine should be a human science not

only because it comes from description of the essence of medical practice but also because the physician-patient relationship is one of caring. According to Pellegrino (1985), care has four meanings in the health professions. The first sense of care is compassion for a fellow human being who is ill. The second is doing for another what he cannot do for himself due to his illness. The third sense of care is when the physician takes responsibility for treating the patient's medical problem using professional knowledge and skill. The fourth sense of caring is taking care of the patient using the craftmanship of medicine (pp. 11–12).

Health care professionals who use the biomedical model of the patient-physician relationship understand the physician's role as encompassing only the third and fourth senses of care. Care in the first two senses is relegated to other health professionals. This bifurcation of health care can be seen most clearly in nursing practice. Traditionally nurses have been involved in patient care in the first two senses. Indeed, nurses traditionally expressed compassion through such direct care for the patient as bathing. Recently, some nurses have seen their role as primarily assisting the physician in caring in the third and fourth sense, while others continue to favor the traditional forms of care. Currently, nurses are trying to overcome this bifurcation by including all four senses of care in their practice, as evidenced by primary nursing.

Where does curing and medical science fit into the caring approach? Obviously, they are not involved in care in some situations. For example, much health care given by physicians and especially by nurses fits the care approach well, because we do not now know how to cure most diseases. In those cases physicians and nurses have learned how to foster natural healing by simply practicing their craft and not from medical science. Craft learned in this way is similar to acquiring skill in the practice of folk medicine. A sophisticated version of folk medicine is indeed practiced by most persons in dealing with minor illnesses with the aid of their pharmacist. Many people treat themselves with home remedies which they have acquired over time, often through family traditions. But today medical science is making cure an ever-increasing possibility. The fact that care is an essential description of the structure of medical practice in cases where cure is not yet possible does not necessarily mean that an important goal of medicine is not cure.

In fact, if confronted with the choice between effective cure and good personal care, most persons would choose cure. That is, they would prefer an authoritarian, obnoxious, competent physician who would cure them of their disease rather than an incompetent, personable and caring physician. However, making these the alternatives misses the essence of health care. Pellegrino (1985) contends that the physician's *moral* commitment is not only to work for the good of the patient but also to be competent in dealing with the patient's illness. Competency requires that the physician not only has learned his craft from practice but that he knows both the taxonomies and cures which medical science has made possible. For this reason the caring approach to medicine does not put caring and curing in opposition to each other. Instead, a caring approach to health care includes cure, when possible, as an integral part of the physician-patient relationship.

But this relationship is not merely aimed at cure when possible. It also must be based on the patient's personal view of the good life. For example, a physician cannot ethically treat a Jehovah's Witness with a blood transfusion, even though the transfusion might cure his disease or improve his condition. Nor could a physician ethically decide to repair a knee of a pro football player in a way that would ensure that the knee would function normally in everyday activities but would end his career as a running back if another more dangerous operation might restore his ability to play football at the risk of losing functional use of the knee. Obviously, medical science cannot determine these decisions. They must be decided by the patient working with a physician who is morally committed to the patient's well-being.

This moral sense of medicine and nursing is often hidden by allegiance to the profession. This occurs when a professional assumes that the profession creates its own ethics. Professional codes assume common consensus, which is rare in our pluralistic, relativistic society. For this reason, Pellegrino contends that codes of medical ethics are not binding in the way that they once were. But lack of consensus is a practical matter. Pellegrino (1985) directs us to a philosophical issue which is at the heart of the matter. According to Pellegrino, it is not the profession that creates the ethic but the moral commitment that creates the profession. As he puts it, one becomes a professional physician by professing to work for the good of the patient and to have the medical competence to treat the patient's illness. Nursing also results from a profession similar to that of the physician. Thus, the moral sense of medicine and nursing does not come from professional consensus, but instead the profession comes from the moral sense and moral commitment, i.e., professing.

If health care is founded on moral commitment, why is the idea that health care is founded on natural science so pervasive? To answer that question, let us consider a case in which medical science seems to be the foundation of medical practice. A person with no symptoms goes to a public health center for a routine physical examination. A physician in attendance discovers a shadow on the lung during a chest X-ray. A CAT scan reveals that there is, in fact, a serious abnormality in the lung. The patient's symptoms and past history of lung infection indicate a recurrence of the infection but the physician prescribes a bronchoscopy and a needle biopsy to test for the remote possibility of cancer. When the tests prove negative, the physician diagnoses a probably infection and prescribes antibiotics. The antibiotics cure the infection. In the foregoing case, the detection of the symptoms, the testing for cancer, the diagnosis of the disease, and the prescription leading to cure all were to the result of medical science. It would seem, on first examination, that this is a clear example of medical science being the foundation of medical practice. What is omitted from the above description is the fact that although the patient had no symptoms, he requested the physical examination out of concern for his physical well-being. Secondly, he had faith in both the physician's competence and the physician's moral commitment to his well-being. If he had thought that the physician was motivated by his financial well-being or by his desire to bring to the hospital customers needed to maintain the expensive CAT scan machine, it is doubtful he would have gone through with the diagnostic examination, much less treatment. But he also might have refused the diagnostic tests and treatment on other grounds. The tests and treatment might simply be too expensive for him. After all, the possibility of cancer was remote and often infections cure themselves, given time. His decision would rest on whether or not he thought the threat of the illness warranted the sacrifice of money and time. Obviously, many value and contextual factors would be involved in making such a decision. But it is a decision the patient must make, not the physician. The physician can help by pointing out the risks, possible prognosis, and probable costs in time and money. From the above example, it should be evident that while medical science can indeed be the foundation for cure, it cannot be the foundation of health care. Health care practice rests on the desire of the person for health, the moral commitment of the physician and nurse to be competent and to use that competence in the best interest of the patient and on the right of the patient to make the final choice with the physician's and nurse's counsel.

Although medical science can be the foundation for cure, medical science itself cannot be understood only, or even mainly, by natural science. After all, Thomas Kuhn (1970) and others have shown, the practice of science, itself, is an interpretive human activity constructed by human beings from a particular perspective. This human activity attempts to understand that which is not itself a human creation, usually designated as nature. Hume (1965, pp. 317–318) well understood that natural objects and man-made objects could not be understood in the same way. In his *Dialogues Concerning Natural Religion*, he pointed out that when one discovers a house, one could logically infer that an architect had designed it. But when one encounters a natural object, he could make no such inference. Hume spoke to a world which tried to give human explanations to natural objects. We live in a world which tries to give natural explanations to human activities and creations. If we follow Hume's logic, we would not look for natural causes of human creations. Instead, we would look for the purpose or the reason for the human creations. In the case of medical practice, the obvious purpose for its creation is the well-being of ill persons.

Human creations are understood by interpretations of meaningful artifacts and actions and not by theoretical explanations of changes in natural objects based on cause and effect. Science, then, is a human way of understanding cause and effect in natural objects. But scientific activity itself is understood through grasping its meaning. Medical science is the human attempt to understand the natural causes of disease and possible ways of eradicating those diseases and/or minimizing their effects on persons. Medical science, however, is not synonymous with health care practice. Health care practice concerns the relationships of persons in which meaning, rather than cause, is crucial. Illness is grasped in terms of its meaning for human life. The relationship between the physician, nurse, and patient is also understood in terms of meaning. This meaning cannot be understood on the basis of medical competency alone. Indeed, medical competence becomes health care only when directed at the well-being of the patient. The well-being of the patient requires that the physician and nurse consider not only the dictates of competent medical practice but also the religious and moral convictions of the patient and the patient's interpretation of the good life as he wishes to live it. In short, understanding health care practice requires understanding the intentional meaning of a relationship between persons.

Those, like Pellegrino, who use the human science approach to understanding health care, search for its essence in concrete practice. The study of health care practice indicates that health care is primarily a relationship of caring.

Certainly, adequate health care requires use of the contributions of biological and chemical science and medical technology. Unfortunately, this reliance on the natural sciences leads some students of medicine to conclude that medicine is founded on natural science. Indeed, this is a comfortable position because that aspect of medical practice which is clearly related to natural science is both foundational and demonstrable. A shot of penicillin can, in fact, be shown to cure strep throat, and in this case, biochemistry is the foundation of the cure. Unfortunately, human science is neither demonstrable nor foundational in the same conclusive way. The human scientists can only investigate the essence of practice and say to other investigators, "This is the sense of that practice. Isn't it obvious to you that it is?" The reason for this is that the human sciences aim at that which is specifically human, and therefore, not causal. Instead, the human sciences aim at meaning, and in this case, the meaning of health care practice. Health care is essentially a caring relationship concerned with the curing of illness when possible. If cure is not possible, health care is concerned with care that promotes the natural healing of the body. If that is not possible, it supports, comforts, and aids those who must live or die with illness.

Disclosing the meaning of this type of relationship is one of the primary functions of the human sciences. However, the nature of health care usually requires that natural explanations be utilized in disclosing the human sense of health care. For example, a physician tells a patient who has had a severe heart attack that if he wants to live, he must stop smoking two packs of cigarettes a day. The patient interprets the physician's warning to mean that smoking could cause lung cancer and thus should be avoided. He confides to his nurses that he intends to keep on smoking because with his heart there is little likelihood that he would live long enough to die of lung cancer. His nurse interprets the meaning of the physician's warning by explaining to the patient that smoking constricts the blood vessels, thus inhibiting the flow of blood to the heart muscle. Obviously, an adequate treatment of health care often requires that the human sciences incorporate the explanations of natural science in their disclosure of the meaning of practice.

Fortunately, Edmund Husserl (1911–1965), the founder of phenomenology, defines the human sciences in a way which can incorporate explanations from the natural sciences. Husserl first defines human science without considering natural science.

> In these sciences theoretical interest is directed exclusively to human beings as persons, to their personal life and activity, as also correlatively to the concrete results of this activity. To live as a person is to live in a social framework, wherein I and we live together in community and have the community as horizon . . . Here the word 'live' is not to be taken in a physiological sense but rather as signifying purposeful living, manifesting spiritual creativity—in the broadest sense, creating culture within historical continuity. It is this that forms the theme of various humanistic sciences (p. 150).

Husserl's definition implies that health care should be studied specifically as a human endeavor as it is lived in the world. But this does not mean that human scientists can ignore what the natural sciences disclose about man. Indeed, Husserl (1911–1965) contends that "the practitioners of the humanistic sciences consider not only the spirit as spirit but must also go back to its bodily foundations" (p. 152). Husserl also recognized that scientific explanation was essential to modern medicine.

> We can illustrate this in terms of the well-known distinction between scientific medicine and "naturopathy." Just as in the common life of peoples the latter derives from naive experience and tradition, so scientific medicine results from the utilization of insights belonging to purely theoretical sciences concerned with the human body, primarily anatomy and physiology. These in turn are based on those fundamental sciences that seek a universal explanation of nature as such, physics and chemistry (Husserl, 1911–1965, p. 149).

Certainly in health care the bodily foundation is crucial to the understanding of health care practice. One cannot understand the meaning of health care practice without understanding its bodily foundations. These bodily foundations are essential to understanding attempts to cure. But health care itself cannot be understood merely as an attempt to cure patients through medical science, because health care is founded on a moral relationship between an ill person and the physician and nurse who profess to care for that person. They profess to be competent in medical science and in the craft (art) of medical and nursing practice. But this profession alone could not make sense of health care practice apart from the moral imperative to use their understanding and skill to promote the physical and psychological well-being of their patients. Promoting the well-being of their patient requires inclusion of their religious, moral, and personal values in therapeutic decisions. Both the medically right and the morally good can be included in the decision when, following Husserl, the bodily foundations of cure explained by the natural sciences are incorporated into an interpretation of health care as a moral relationship between physician, nurse, and patient whose meaning is disclosed by the human sciences.

Chapter 4

The Sense of Nursing: Applied Science or Practical Human Science?

Health care, being a human activity, is most appropriately studied by the human sciences as we have shown in the previous chapter. But what kind of human science is most appropriate for the study of health care and what is the alternative to studying it as human science? We will contend that health care is a human practice and that the study of that practice should be designated as a practical human science. We will reject the alternative claim that health care is an applied science which is appropriately studied by the behavioral sciences. However, we will also contend that, unlike the other practical human sciences, the study of health care must be able to show how natural science can be applied to health care practice, as Husserl contends, without transforming it from a human practice to an applied science.

When nursing is treated as an applied science, it usually has two senses. In the first sense nursing becomes a technology inferred from medical science. In the second sense nursing practice is reordered using the theories of those behavioral sciences which copy the natural sciences. In contrast to imitating the natural sciences, the human sciences study man in ways particularly appropriate to human being in the world. We will show how human science can articulate nursing practice from within nursing itself and can, through the hermeneutic spiral, productively use the theories of the natural and behavioral sciences to understand and improve nursing practice without transforming it into an applied science or technology.

The fundamental issue concerns whether nursing itself is constituted as a practice in the lived world or as an applied science derived from the natural sciences. It does not concern whether the human sciences or the natural sciences are needed to understand nursing practice. Obviously, both are needed. The human sciences can articulate nursing practice because the human sciences study the meaning of human actions, expressions, social organizations and practices. In contrast, the natural sciences are concerned with general facts derived from theoretical explanations of natural phenomena. For example, a patient suffers an attack of hypoglycemia. The patient's husband calls the nurse; the nurse, knowing the patient's medical history, recognizes the problem and explains to the husband that the patient is suffering from hypoglycemia or low blood sugar. The husband is surprised when she feeds the patient cheese and asks, "Why did you not give her sugar?" She answers that sugar causes the pancreas to release more insulin, which would magnify the problem. She has used a theoretical explanation to help the patient grasp the meaning of her actions. In contrast, a patient who has had a breast biopsy is advised by her nurse to call for help before attempting to get out of bed to go to the bathroom. The patient indignantly responds that she is perfectly capable of taking care of herself. The nurse points out that after general anesthesia patients often experience dizziness when they get up for the first time. This interpretation of the nurse's action is based on previous experience and not on scientific explanation. Although there is a scientific explanation for dizziness, nurses know about dizziness from practical experience, and it is that experience which usually informs their practice rather than scientific explanation, as in the case of hypoglycemia. Thus, the meaning of a nurse's behavior can be given through a scientific theoretical explanation or through an interpretation of practice.

Both interpretation of practice and theoretical explanation are necessary to make sense of nursing practice. However, as we have shown in the previous chapter, both the descriptions of illness and the physician-patient relationship are interpretations of practical experience. Scientific explanation becomes necessary when illness is treated as disease and when certain medical procedures are explained. Thus, the sense of nursing is based on practical experience that is enhanced by theoretical scientific explanation when it is needed without reducing practice to an applied science or technology.

Practical and Applied Science

When practice is reduced to applied science or technology, humans are theoretically designated as objects, which denies their humanity by reducing them to things entirely determined by natural forces. Natural science, itself, does not necessarily reduce humans to objects. Instead, it focuses on that aspect of human being which is natural; namely, the organic. Before the advent of the behavioral sciences, the human aspect of human being was studied by the humanities. However, when the behavioral sciences adopted the methodology and assumptions of the natural sciences, the peaceful co-existence between the sciences and humanities ended. Human beings were made the objects of theoretical study designed to explain human behavior in terms of cause and effect.

Strasser (1985) shows how human beings can be studied theoretically without copying the methodology and assumptions of the natural sciences. He contends that there are two kinds of theory, one appropriate for the natural sciences, the other for the human sciences. The first is concerned with the pursuit of truth and the second with articulation and improvement of practice. Natural science has its own particular way which involves "thinking and speaking logically and systematically" (Strasser, 1985, p 58) in pursuit of truth by using such methods as "observation, experimentation, measuring, calculating, etc." (p. 58). Also, natural science uses theory to explain natural things as objects. In contrast, human science uses theory to articulate the practices of the lifeworld which have "extra-scientific aims" (p. 58). Strasser points out that this distinction is often blurred. For example, a medical scientist invents a new medicine to cure a disease. The evaluation of that medicine occurs both through scientific experimentation and through medical practice. The experimentation is to test the truth of the proposed cure. Use in practice evaluates the cure in terms of the good at which medical practice aims, namely improving or restoring the health of an ill person.

The latter is designated as a practical science by Strasser in order to distinguish it from an applied science. According to Strasser (1985) a *"practical science is a science which is conceived in order to make possible, to improve, and to correct a definite kind of extra-scientific praxis"* (p. 59). In contrast, applied sciences are sciences "which are *accidentally applied* to a practical context" (p. 59). The key terms in these two definitions are "conceived in order to" and "accidentally applied." For example, a nurse who works on a unit with a high incidence of decubitus ulcers may decide to experiment with nursing practice in order to develop procedures which prevent the occurrence of decubitus ulcers. This is an example of a practical human science. On the other hand, a nurse would engage in applied science if she infers procedures for preventing decubitus ulcers from knowledge obtained from a research report by a biologist, who had discovered that poor circulation has a detrimental effect on skin integrity. Pure examples like the foregoing are useful in making distinctions but are rare in actual health care practice. In actual practice, nurses are more apt to begin with actual problems like the decubitus ulcer and then draw on theoretical knowledge for understanding and inferring direction. But the solution which improves practice usually can only be worked out during and through practice. Later, following Strasser, we will call this movement from practice to theory and back to practice a hermeneutic spiral.

A central issue in present-day health care is whether nursing and other health care professions are practices in their own right or are applied sciences. In contrast to Benner's study of nursing excellence which affirms nursing practice, treating nursing as an applied science denies the legitimacy of traditional nursing practice by using the theories of the social or behavioral sciences to dictate what nursing is to be. For example, much of the stress on competencies stated as behavioral objectives in nursing education has resulted from the application of behaviorists' psychological theories to nursing. Thus, what constitutes competency has been determined from outside practice. Benner, on the other hand, approaches competency from within concrete nursing practice. The thrust of her whole book indicates that nursing is a practice and not an applied discipline.

Benner further shows that know-how derived from practice often runs ahead of and challenges the knowledge of scientific theory. She does this in the context of distinguishing between theoretical and practical knowledge. Theoretical knowledge is "knowing that" while practical knowledge is "knowing how" (Benner, 1984, p. 3). However, when one speaks of an applied discipline, it usually means that the knowing how is derived from the knowing that. In contrast, practical knowledge usually means "that knowledge that accrues over time" (p. 1) from practice. By articulating nursing from within, practical human science can make an important contribution to the understanding of nursing, as Benner has so convincingly shown.

Can applied science adequately describe nursing? If nursing is an applied science, then it is a technology. Technology uses science as a means of effecting some human goal, not as a pursuit of the truth. According to Strasser (1985), the "*one* value which dominates the totality of technological thought" is efficiency. Therefore he defines technology as "the science of the means as such" (p. 61). Since "the evaluation of the efficiency of a means depends on the end which should be reached" (p. 62), it is "impossible to specify in a universally valid manner the criteria which are decisive for the evaluation of technical means" (p. 62). For example, medical science may develop an efficient means for keeping a comatose body alive, but it cannot judge whether the body should be kept alive.

In technology, results can be measured. For example, one can determine by measurement whether or not a human being is alive. The measurement of brain waves is now considered an adequate determiner of life or death, but prior to the advent of such measurements, other measurements such as blood pressure and breathing were used to determine life or death. All that has changed is efficiency in the determination of life or death. But it is impossible to determine by measurement what quality of human life warrants keeping someone alive, much less what constitutes physical or mental health. Since technology obviously cannot deal with values other than efficiency, it cannot tell us of the undesirable effects of a means. It is especially important to recognize this limitation when using the human sciences. For example, one nursing textbook states: "Behavioristic strategies are also useful tools to nurses working with physically disabled clients in rehabilitation" (Johnson, 1986, p. 21). There is no indication that such strategies as token rewards may develop dependencies on receiving rewards for accomplishments or may undermine personal moral achievement. For example, such a system was installed for all the patients in an institution for the mentally retarded. This system fostered dependency and a lower sense of values in many of the more intelligent patients who had tended to care for themselves out of the sense of their own worth. Since means directed toward one end often have other unintended results, it is essential that the use of medical science and technology in health care be incorporated within practices in which the moral sense is dominant.

Hermeneutic Spiral

The hermeneutic spiral, as developed by Strasser (1985), makes it possible to begin with interpretations of practical experience and then to use theoretical explanations to both better understand that experience and to use that understanding to improve practice. Strasser points out that traditionally the human sciences have been distinguished from the natural sciences in that the human sciences seek understanding, whereas the natural sciences aim at causal explanations. Further, understanding is gained through interpretation whereas explanations are sought through theory. Strasser argues for a hermeneutic spiral in which one first interprets experiences or practices, then uses explanations to assist in coming to an understanding and then brings that understanding to bear again on the original experience or practice.

In health care two kinds of theory are brought to bear on practice—natural science theory and human science theory. The following is an example of the use of natural science theory in understanding nursing practice. A very important aspect of nursing care for a patient with stroke is to protect the integrity of the skin. In order to protect the integrity of the skin, the nurse must turn the patient frequently. Patients often resist frequent turning and ask why it is necessary that they be moved so often. The nurse can help the patient to understand the necessity for frequent turning by explaining that when pressure continues on a particular area of the skin for a long period, the circulation of the skin is impaired, thus causing the skin to break down. Further explanations about the severity of skin breakdown and the possible development of a decubitus ulcer will aid in understanding what might seem a worrisome bother to the patient—to change position every hour or two. It gives the patient an understanding of possible consequences to his own body if he fails to cooperate with frequent turning. This is a simple example of a hermeneutic spiral. It is hermeneutic in that a nursing procedure, turning the patient, is interpreted to the patient. The process begins with a concrete nursing practice which is explained in terms of scientific theory concerning the relationship of circulation to skin integrity. In the spiral, further conversation between nurse and patient open up the possibility for the patient to accept responsibility for protecting the integrity of his own skin by cooperating in turning or by turning without assistance or supervision if he is able.

The hermeneutic spiral is especially significant because health care practice requires the continual relationship of theory to practice and of practice to the everyday life of the patient. We selected the above example because in that example these relationships were clear, simple, and direct. In another example a patient brings to a physician the description of his illness as it affects his everyday life. The physician uses his expert theoretical knowledge of medicine to resignify the illness as a disease for which he can prescribe treatment. The recommended treatment is shared through dialogue with the patient in everyday language. The physician discusses with the patient the possible consequences of recommended treatment. The outcome might be a return to his life as it was, an improved life, a more restricted life or less suffering at the end of live. At any rate, from this more adequate understanding, the patient is able to engage in a dialogue in which the physician brings his theoretical understanding to bear on the patient's illness and prospects. At some place in this spiral of increased understanding, they must arrive at a decision concerning treatment. In the past the hermeneutic spiral often was carried on by the physician, himself, in that the physician moved from the patient's description of illness to an understanding of illness as disease, usually through theory, to prescriptions concerning treatment of disease which would hopefully restore the patient's health. The patients' rights movement and the current stress on the moral responsibilities of the physician makes the spiral especially appropriate for enhancing the patient's understanding of his illness so that the physician and patient can come to a mutual decision concerning treatment. Also, the current emphasis on team decisions concerning treatment and care makes the spiral important for the nurse in developing a plan of care with patient and physician.

In the above examples, scientific theory was used in understanding health care practice and in reaching decisions concerning treatment and care. But the theories often used in the hermeneutic spiral are taken from the human sciences. Strasser gives the following example of such a spiral. He describes a therapist attempting to help a young woman resolve her antagonism to her mother. In the first phase the therapist listens patiently, attentively, and sympathetically as the young woman describes her quarrels with her mother and the tensions in the home resulting from those quarrels. In the second phase, the therapist inquires about the daughter's relationship with her father and discovers that the young woman is evasive and reluctant to discuss her relationship with her father. In the third phase the therapist applies Freud's theory of the Oedipal complex to the daughter's problems in relating to her mother, which helps explain the daughter's difficulties. In the fourth phase, the practical phase, the therapist helps his patient understand the subconscious drives that foster tensions between herself and her mother (Strasser, 1985, pp. 22–24). When the patient and the therapist again address the tensions between mother and daughter, it will be from the vantage point of this increased understanding. This example shows how theory can be helpful in the understanding of human behavior. But it also indicates that one should begin by attempting to understand human behavior as it appears in everyday experience before theory is brought to bear on it and, after theoretical explanation, must return to everyday experience.

The previous example begins at one level of understanding and the use of theory brings it to a higher level of understanding. The daughter first understands her relationship to her mother as one of tension; then she comes to understand these tensions in a different way through the theory of the Oedipal complex. But for the new understanding to operate as therapy, she must incorporate it into her tensive relations with her mother in a way that transforms the relationship.

The patient's recovery requires establishing new relationships with her mother. Thus, understanding the underlying reason for her tensions with her mother is merely the first step in her therapy. The next step which restores the patient to the lived world might be done by the psychiatric nurse. In the above case, this would be done by helping the patient find ways to lessen or eliminate the tension with her mother. Although the psychotherapist might terminate the therapy when the young woman gained new understanding through psychotherapy, the psychiatric nurse would continue it by attempting to get the patient to relate to her mother in a new way. The nurse believes the tension will continue because she has learned from communication theory and from her own observations in similar situations that people continue to communicate in habitual ways which have developed in tensive relationships. She recognizes the anger that typically occurs when these patterns of communication appear in conversations between mother and daughter. Through counseling and role play, she helps both become aware of the ways that foster tension and anger and helps them develop new ways of communicating.

Notice that in this continuation of the hermeneutic spiral, it makes no difference whether the nurse's insight into communication comes from the theory of an expert in communications or from her reflection on her own practice. What is essential is that the hypothesis not be used to prescribe practice. Instead, the spiral begins with practice, theory or reflection enlightens it, and returns to practice by enhancing it.

Without the hermeneutic spiral, theory is used prescriptively in a way that reduces or distorts human experience. For example, psychoanalytic theory could distort rather than enlighten the daughter's tensions with her mother if they had not been, in part, caused by an Oedipal complex. Failing to recognize this in the past, many psychoanalysts used psychoanalytic theory in a prescriptive and reductive way. They believed not only that psychoanalysis was the only way to understand mental illness and that it was the only adequate way to treat illness, but that Freudian psychology gave an adequate account of human experience. In the hermeneutic spiral, psychoanalysis is merely regarded as one theory among others which might contribute to understanding a particular patient's mental illness. The test of its appropriateness is not that it conforms to psychoanalytic theory but that the theory fosters understanding of the patient's experience and opens up new possibilities for a better life. The use of theory in the hermeneutic spiral is very different from that in applied science. Applied science uses theory to determine methods and procedures. To their credit many nursing theorists have stopped short of contending that theories drawn from the natural and/or social sciences should determine nursing practice. But the consequence of not following the logic of an applied science is often confusing. For example, this ambiguity is clearly illustrated in Betty Neuman's (1982) attempt to apply systems theory to nursing. She believes that systems theory will bring unity to nursing practice which has been fractured by specialization. But she fails to show how this could be accomplished in any concrete way. Obviously, her understanding of the problem comes from interpreting practice, as do many of her astute suggestions for improving nursing. What is unclear is how systems theory relates to nursing practice. If Neuman applies systems theory to nursing prescriptively, then nursing practice would be formed or structured by that theory. On the other hand, if she uses systems theory in a hermeneutic spiral, it would be used to understand the problem of disunity in contemporary nursing practice and to point out possible sources of wholeness in that practice.

Unfortunately, theory is often prescriptive because the social and behavioral sciences often copy the way theory is used in the natural sciences. Strasser contends that such use of theory objectifies and reduces human experience. For this reason, he contends that human science theory must begin with human experience, be appropriate to human experience, and test its adequacy against human experience.

Theory in the Human Sciences

Since theory must be appropriate for the human experience, it can not be universal and determinative in the way in which the theory of gravitation and Newton's second law can predict exactly and without exception the speed at which any object will fall to the earth. According to Strasser

(1985), theory in the human sciences does not aim at universal truth but at general truth. For Strasser, human science theory uses general propositions to elucidate "systematically and critically *a definite section of reality viewed from a definite standpoint*" (pp. 34–35). But use of general propositions should not exclude the uniqueness of the particular human being studied. For example, theories of child development help nurses understand the behavior of "the terrible two's." But such understanding will not tell them how a particular child will respond to this stage of development or how a particular nurse can work concretely with this child. If this theory had the universality of theories in the natural sciences, one would be able to predict exactly how any child going through this stage would act, and it could be used to develop a technology which would tell any nurse how to control his behavior. However, any theory appropriate to the human sciences must take into account human agency and the uniqueness of particular human relationships.

The natural sciences can give universal explanations because they treat objects completely determined by natural forces. Therefore, they are concerned with what Strasser (1985) calls thing-objects in contrast to the human sciences which treat thing-subjects. Behaviorists, following the natural science model, treat humans as *any* organism and therefore eliminate such aspects of human being as meaning and values. In addition, they follow the natural sciences' use of deductive, physical law explanations which rule out the possibility of voluntary action. In contrast, the human sciences deal with man as an active agent, capable of communication and action, thus as a cooperating object and co-subject. For this reason, Strasser (1985) uses the term subject-object to refer to the objects of human science theory. In so doing, he does not reduce persons to objects but merely makes the point that when persons are studied with human science theory, they are treated in a general way rather than a particular way. Incorporating theory within the hermeneutic spiral which begins and ends with the experience of particular persons precludes prescriptive use of theory, which reduces persons to objects.

Strasser further defines human science theory by contrasting the way it treats man with the way in which natural science theory treats man. In the natural sciences man is treated as a product of nature, as an organism dependent on biological environment. Thus man is studied as any other natural object. But objectified man is radically different from the subject (the scientist) studying man as object. In contrast, the human sciences view man as the originator and organizer of his surrounding world. Thus when a human scientist studies the development of the socio-cultural world, he studies man as a human subject like himself. Of course, in his studies he often views man from a theoretical perspective but it is nevertheless one which recognizes that human beings are not mere objects but rather subject-objects. Thus, when he communicates with others, he speaks to them as fellow symbolic human beings. Strasser summarizes this as "natural science proceeds by way of *objectification through reification*, human science by way of *objectification through communication*" (p. 68).

When theories are used to account for human behavior, in a general way, one is apt to forget that any such explanation begins with and depends on understanding the everyday world. Husserl (1911–1965) pointed out that the sciences live in forgetfulness of their dependence on the everyday world. After all, there were trees before there were botanists. If there had not been trees and other plants in our everyday world, there certainly would have been no botanists. Likewise, there was nursing care in the family and elsewhere long before there was professional nursing. Florence Nightingale originated the modern profession of nursing by articulating, expanding, and developing nursing care. Nursing grew out of everyday nursing care rather than out of theoretical or practical medicine. However, over time theoretical and practical medicine have greatly influenced nursing practice. Currently, nurses are seeking theories of nursing to give direction to practice. But the question of how these theories relate to practice is a perplexing one. Some theorists seek them in the natural, behavioral, and/or social sciences. These theories are then *applied* to nursing. Thus theory determines practice and "practice" becomes an inappropriate name for technology. Such an approach neglects Husserl's insight that all sciences themselves are originally dependent on everyday experience. In everyday experience, health care does not begin from the desire to apply theory to practice, although some professors in schools of nursing sometimes give this impression. Nursing begins with the desire to care for the ill in order to comfort them, lessen their suffering, and/or restore them to a normal life. While theoretical studies of health care can lose sight of this original intention, they should not do so because health care, itself, is practical rather than theoretical.

Practical and Theoretical Human Sciences

Health care, according to Strasser (1985), is one of the practical human sciences. He identifies three types of human science—practical, theoretical, and theoretical with practical aspects. All of these human sciences have three common traits. One, human scientists communicate with the subject-objects they study; two, they do not use theory to reduce humans to object-objects; and third, they consider themselves "part of the social, historical, cultural world which they study" (p. 73).

Strasser distinguishes the three types from each other based upon their style of communication and their aim. He defines theoretical human science as studies based on "*the understanding and the interpretation of symbols and systems of symbols*: languages, written documents, works of art, political, cultural, political institutions, etc." (p. 73). These sciences, philology, linguistics, history, archeology, and cultural anthropology, have as their primary aim the "scientific description of the social, cultural, historical world or some of its sections" (p. 73).

Practical human science is based on communicative action which presupposes direct participation in some kind of praxis. These human sciences—health care, psychotherapy, education, political science, and criminology—all have as their aim the articulation and improvement of these practices. Thus they share with practitioners the responsibility for the future development of these practices.

The third type of human science is one which combines both the theoretical and practical in one human science in that they are partly aimed at describing social life and partly aimed at improving it. These sciences include economics, sociology and psychology.

From Strasser's descriptions of the human sciences, it is evident that health care would be a practical human science, in that it is "intent on continuation, improvement, and correction of typical forms of interpersonal praxis for the sake of specific human values" (Strasser, 1985, p. 76). Two typical forms of interpersonal praxis are the practices of medicine and of nursing which have as their purpose fostering the physical and psychological well-being of the patient. But even when the moral sense is dominant—promoting the physical and/or psychological well-being of the patient—practitioner and human scientist may have different immediate aims. The practitioner is interested in healing the ill while the human scientist's goal is studying the practice through which this occurs. Their common shared long range aim of promoting the well-being of patient does not guarantee harmonious collaboration. Practitioners focus so much on immediate ends, like lowering the blood pressure, that it is easy to lose sight of the importance of understanding and improving practice. The same is true of practical human scientists who frequently become so absorbed in studying the processes of the practice that they forget that the purpose of the research is to improve practice. When practitioners and researchers are not explicitly conscious of the moral sense which founds their practice, they tend to get lost in the techniques and immediate activities of their practice.

Tensions between practitioners and human scientists can also result from different intentionalities rather than from losing sight of the long range goal. For example, a

nurse's aim is to foster the healing of the patient. A human
scientist would study the process of fostering the healing of
the patient. Most practical human scientists tend to believe
that they improve nursing practice through helping nurses
better to understand the process and to discover possibilities for improving it. Thus, a human scientist would
share the moral imperative of the nurse to foster healing.
However, unlike the nurse, the human scientist would also
have an equal commitment to the pursuit of truth, which
although not necessarily shared with the nurse, is after all
a moral imperative. Is the pursuit of truth without a commitment to the improvement of practice an adequate commitment for studying the practical human sciences? For
example, the sociologist might study the role of the nurse
in a hospital without having any commitment to the improvement of nursing. Benner (1984), in fact, claims that
"nursing practice has been studied primarily from the
sociological perspective. Thus, we have learned much about
role relationships, socialization, and acculturation in nursing practice" (p. 1). But this knowledge does not necessarily
improve practice. In fact, one reason for the oft-made charge
that government and private grants given to academic departments for such studies rarely result in improved practice is that those making the studies have little commitment to the improvement of practice. Scholarship collected
with purely academic motives is usually not organized or
presented in ways which speak to, much less foster, improved practice. Ideally, practical human scientists in health
care should have a dual commitment to the truth and to improvement of practice.

Health care practitioners should also share the re-
searcher's goals of articulating and improving practice. Certainly, an excellent nurse attempts to make sense of what
she is doing, and her practice reflects that understanding. In
addition, she looks for possible ways of improving practice
and incorporates those ways into her practice and shares
them with others. When health care practitioners and human scientists share each other's intentionalities, then good

patient care, understanding that care, and improving it come together in a common enterprise.

Often in the practical human sciences, the theorist-researcher is also a practitioner. This is in sharp contrast to the natural sciences in which theory formation and technological application are completely separate activities. Those who advocate this separation in health care should consider that many, if not most, of the significant theorist and researchers in health care have been physicians and nurses. Indeed, it would be difficult to think of an outstanding theorist in psychotherapy who was not a practitioner, i.e., Freud, Jung, May, Rogers, and Sullivan.

Although it is obvious that practitioners and human scientists should share the same goals of articulating and improving practice, it is not evident that the practice of nursing is, itself, a human science. Strasser, himself, is unclear whether he believes health care practice, itself, is a human science or the study of it constitutes a human science. However, he does state that human science studies health care in order to improve it and therefore is a practical human science. But does this mean that a practicing nurse or physician is necessarily engaged in practical human science? Although articulating and improving practice are important aspects of excellent practice, practice, itself, focuses on caring for ill persons and fostering their physical and psychological well-being. Certainly, it would not be good practice for a surgeon or the nurse assisting him to be thinking about articulating and improving practice while engaged in triple by-pass surgery. Our point is that the aim of medicine and nursing is primarily care for the ill and not primarily the study of that care. However, appropriate study of that care is essential to understanding and improving it. For achieving the latter, the practical human sciences are especially well-suited.

The applied sciences do improve health care practice, but they do so instrumentally. Strasser makes this evident in distinguishing between science and applied science. Science aims at the discovery of truth, whereas, medical science has the "extra-scientific" purpose of healing. Applied sciences are sciences "which are *accidentally applied* to a practical context" (p. 59). By accidental he means that the original purpose of the scientific investigation was not to improve health care, but someone used it to improve health care. The discovery of penicillin would be an obvious example of applied science. However, a counter example would be a biochemist whose pursuit of truth concerns mutation in cells but who has chosen this specialty because he hopes his discoveries will contribute to developing a cure for cancer. It seems odd to designate this high moral purpose as "extra-scientific" and "accidentally applied." This odd designation is the consequence of Strasser's beginning with science and making definitions in contrast to science. It would be much clearer if Strasser had said some human beings engage in activities such as pure science which seeks to understand the world; others in such activities as health care practice which directly fosters human good. The scientist in the foregoing example is using understanding to foster human good. What makes it an applied science is that he *uses* science to improve health care. Applied science is always instrumental.

In contrast to applied science, which is instrumental, human science aims at understanding specific human activities. The practical human sciences seek to understand those practices which directly foster human good. The purpose in such study is to improve practice through understanding. The practical human sciences help practitioners understand the meaning of what they are engaged in by providing a context of understanding within which practice can be more meaningfully pursued and improved.

Strasser illustrates how the practical human sciences can improve practice by understanding its essence and realizing its possibilities. Nursing and medicine are practices which use applied science. Strasser shows through the hermeneutic spiral how medical science and technology can be applied to practice without making it an applied science. The hermeneutic spiral can also incorporate the theories of the human sciences and behavioral sciences into health care practice, especially nursing, without the reification and objectification of applied science. Thus, Strasser helps distinguish human practice from applied science and shows how they can be related to each other without transforming practice into applied science. In so doing, he makes evident the folly of the recent tendency to transform successful ongoing practices, such as nursing, into applied sciences. But unfortunately, he follows the modern tendency to begin with science and its application to human ends and treats the human sciences as ways of understanding those aspects of human being which elude science and technology. As important as Strasser's contributions are for understanding nursing practice, an adequate understanding requires a positive study of human practice as it is found in the lived world and reflected on in a philosophy of practice.

Chapter 5

Nursing and Philosophy of Practice

A practical human science is a study of human practice. Medical practice has traditionally been used to describe the vocation physicians engage in. One physician defined his medical practice as "the care I give to those persons who are my patients." He was not sure that nursing had been a practice in the 1950s when his wife, who had been a nurse, began working in hospitals. But he thought that the change that had taken place in nursing since then might qualify it as practice. However, the changes he mentioned resulted primarily from medical technology. One of his examples was nurses in coronary care units who, on the basis of expert understanding, make crucial decisions about patient care without consulting a physician. He did add, however, that they did so under the general direction of a physician. Note that for him nurses become professionals, not only by attaining self-direction, but by becoming more like medical technicians than traditional nurses who give nursing care to their patients.

Benner's (1984) study of nursing competencies clearly shows that nursing is a practice with its own competencies derived from the practice of nursing itself. In addition, she shows that this practice requires movement from a novice stage to an expert stage. We have also shown that nursing practice includes functioning in-between physician, patient, and hospital administration and that it has a moral sense as its foundation.

Certainly, Florence Nightingale established nursing as

a practice independent of medicine. She clearly understood
that the rise of medical science posed a threat to the integrity of nursing practice. This was one of the reasons she opposed the new germ theory of disease and of contagion as
Charles Rosenberg (1979) has clearly shown.

> On the practical level, moreover, it threatened the future
> of nursing as a profession; if prudence, proper regimen,
> and good general health could not protect against conta-
> gion, then nursing must be a perilous trade indeed (p. 127).

However, Rosenberg also shows that in spite of Nightingale's rejecting the theory of contagion, as did many physicians of her time, her views on actual nursing practice were
sound and later were supported by the theory of germs and
contagion. Certainly, this demonstrates that sound nursing
practice can develop on its own.

Nightingale did grasp that advances in medical science
and technology could pose a threat to the integrity of nursing practice, however. Strasser shows us the reason for this
threat both to nursing and medical practice. If medical or
nursing practice is dictated primarily by medical science,
then both nursing and medicine become applied science.
But Strasser affords us a means of using medical science to
improve practice *without* transforming it to applied science
through the use of the hermeneutic spiral. For example, had
Nightingale used the hermeneutic spiral, which of course
was unknown in her time, the theory of germs and contagion would not have been a threat to nursing care. She knew
from practice that a proper hospital environment, including
good ventilation, proper diet, cleanliness, and patient hy-
giene fostered healing and helped prevent the spread of disease. If she had applied the theory of germs and contagion
to her sound practice, it would have explained why her practice worked. In addition, working out the implication of
these theories would have actually improved nursing practice, thus having a spiral effect. The hermeneutic spiral
would also account for how the physician, who doubted
that nursing had been a practice, could define practice as
care for his patients and at the same time use the latest med-

ical science and technology in that practice in the way that he actually did. Thus, medical science and technology can improve nursing and medical practice without making it an applied science.

The Degeneration of Practice into Technique

When applied medical science replaces practice, practice degenerates into technique. Nursing is primarily a practice which has traditionally been concerned with caring for the ill in such a way as to foster comfort and healing. Like all practices, it has been passed on from one generation to the next, first in an apprentice relationship and later through clinical experiences. Recently, the use of the scientific model in which theory determines technique has been advocated by academic and professional leaders in nursing. This approach has its roots in those social and behavioral sciences which copy the natural sciences and not in nursing practice itself. Often this approach is used to gain academic respectability by copying the social and even natural sciences. But such approaches neglect the fact that nursing is a practice and ought to be studied as such.

Gadamer (1976–1981) helps us to understand that this "degeneration of practice into technique" is a wide-spread phenomenon in Western society. He points out that most Westerners think of practice as opposed to theory; in addition, they think of practice as an application of science. This opposition between theory and practice would have been unthinkable to the classical Greek philosophers. To them, *theoria* meant "the eye disciplined enough to discern the visably structured order . . . of the world and of human society" (p. 69). Obviously, a theory of practice would discern the order which gives meaning to the practice. As such, it could hardly be opposed to practice!

Gadamer (1976–1981) also points out that science is very different for moderns than it was for the Greeks. For the Greeks, science focused on that which was experienceable in the everyday world and was worth knowing. In the modern world, scientific theory has lost its connection with what is worth knowing and has ceased to focus on the "primarily experienceable and familiar totality of our world." Modern science has become "knowledge of manipulable relationships by means of isolating experimentation" (p. 70). Further, manipulation and experimentation are used to predict outcomes. The ability to predict outcomes has led to the technology which now dominates our lives. When "the hour of technology has arrived by way of science," the "old relationship of the products of the arts and crafts with the models furnished by nature has thus been transformed into an ideal of construction, into the ideal of a nature artificially produced in accord with an idea" (p. 70).

The transformation of which Gadamer speaks is evident in health care. Traditionally health care followed natural ways of healing. Florence Nightingale (1859–1946) noted that neither medicine nor nursing could cure and the function of nursing was to "put the patient in the best condition for nature to act upon him" (p. 75). In fact, health care, including medicine, was primarily concerned with how to evoke and foster the natural process of healing. With the advent of modern scientific medicine, radical cure becomes possible by elimination of disease from the body through drugs and/or surgery. Thus, the natural course of healing is not followed and in some cases is not primarily involved. For example, when parts of the ear or eye are replaced with plastic, those parts have not been naturally healed but replaced. The spectacular results of this scientific-technical appproach to medicine has led many professionals to think of this as *the* model for medicine. If this is the case, then medicine becomes an applied science and physicians become medical technologists and nurses, at best, become technicians, and, at worst, appliers of techniques developed by medical technicians.

This threatened reduction in the status of nursing is in accord with the general trends of the technological society as Gadamer sees them. In a technological society, the experts make practical, political, and economic decisions for us. A consequence of this turn to technology is the loss of personal identity by the elevation of "adaptive qualities to privileged status" (Gadamer, 1976–1981, p. 73). This is evident in the attempt of nursing to maintain an identity with the rise of technicians such as respiratory therapists, physical therapists, and occupational therapists. Nurses have had to adapt to the constant changes in medical science and technology and to the new ways of thinking and the procedures they have engendered. Indeed, the frantic search for a theory of nursing is an attempt to establish an identity in a time of rapid technological change which threatens the older established *practice* of nursing.

Replacing practice with technique not only threatens the identity of nursing but makes it impossible for the nurse to establish her identity by making choices within her chosen profession. Instead of choices she would merely apply techniques developed by others under the assumption that techniques chosen by experts will result in the good for the patient. Thus, she would not be practicing the art or profession of nursing. Nurses should heed the comment of Pellegrino (1985) that many people who are called physicians, are, in fact, really health care technicians. The difference between a technician and a professional is that a technician uses techniques which are evaluated by efficiency; whereas, the professional makes decisions which are evaluated by the good. Pellegrino reminds us that profession means that one professes to be able to help another. A professional not only makes choices affecting the good of the other, but in making those choices, also affects his own being and thus contributes his own identity.

The ability to choose, in part, one's own identity and to make choices affecting one's own world is unique to man. Man, according to Gadamer (1976–1981), "has spiraled out of the order of nature" by turning "against the natural vital instincts of survival" (p. 75). When man is able to forego the satisfying of immediate needs, labor is possible. The development of language makes possible the pursuit of remote goals in cooperation with other humans. When man no longer is guided by instinctive needs and drives, "there is a need for enlightened choice, just deliberation, and right subordination under common ends" (p.

76). These decisions are moral decisions in that they concern right and wrong.

> In contrast to animals where collective behavior is used to adapt to natural conditions, man's social behavior is aimed at a common good. Human society is organized for the sake of a common order to living, so that each individual knows and acknowledges it as a common one (and even in its breakdowns, in crime). It is precisely the excess beyond what is necessary for the mere preservation of life that distinguishes his action as human action (Gadamer, 1976–1981, pp. 76–77).

Human action directed by communal ways of being, aimed at promoting human good, is the essence of what Gadamer means by practice. Thus, although nursing is sometimes concerned with natural survival, the practice of nursing itself is not a natural but a human achievement. Its final goal is more than mere human survival in that it aims at human well-being.

The dominant sense of practice for Gadamer is obviously a moral sense. However, this moral sense must be made concrete. Achieving the good requires more than wishing for it, according to Gadamer (1976–1981).

> It is the creative capacity of human beings to come up with wishes and to try to find ways to satisfy them, but that does not change the fact that wishing is not willing; it is not practice. Practice consists of choosing, of deciding for something and against something else, and in doing this a practical reflection is effective (p. 81).

Practical reflection requires thinking about how to bring about what I will. "If I will this, then I must have that; if I want to have this, then I have to have this . . . ; until at last I come back to my own situation, where I myself can take things in hand" (Gadamer, 1976–1981, p. 81). For example, a nurse practitioner wants to practice in an inner city where there is no health care. First, she has to seek the assistance of a physician with whom to work. If she wants to work with a physician, she must find one who is concerned about the poor and must formulate a plan which will convince the physician to work with her. Thus, she returns to her own situation and creative resources. Therefore, sound practice requires creative willing which concretizes the possibilities for good inherent in practice.

For Gadamer (1976–1981) practice means acting in communal concert to concretize the common good. This is because practices are the bearers of intentionality that spring from participation in cultural groups with common meanings and values. However, sound practice requires critique in order to improve traditional practice. Critique, for Gadamer, is dialectical rather than utopian or ideal. Dialectical critique requires that the ideal and the actual practice be brought together in such a way that they concretize the possibilities inherent in practice, and thereby improve practice. The appropriateness of Gadamer's dialectical critique is evident to all who have tried to reform practice. Usually reformers are looked upon as unpractical by practitioners because they focus only on the ideal to be achieved and ignore the possibilities for improvement inherent in practice. Sound practice requires critique but critique which takes seriously the requirement of practice in the given community. Reform is thus not prescription from a utopian idea because an ideal "is not a guide for action but a guide for reflection" (p. 82). Practice and how it can be improved by realizing its possibilities is what ought to be reflected upon.

If the aforementioned nurse practitioner follows Gadamer's dialectic criticism, she would be neither a detached critic nor an unpractical idealist. She would concern herself with both criticism of the present situation and with the possibilities in that situation for improved health care for the poor. For example, she would certainly criticize our present health care system which neglects the have-nots and focuses on care for the haves. But in so doing, she would consider the possibilities for the good which are realizable in medical and nursing practice. Further, she would attempt to formulate a plan which would concretize the realization of these possibilities.

Reflection on practice requires theory but not the theory which is opposed to practice. Instead, reflection on practice requires a theory which articulates the practice. The Greek conception of theory, as Gadamer points out, was different from modern theory, which concerns techniques that are evaluated in terms of fulfilling their purposes. Instead of being utilitarian, Greek theory addressed the standards of deciding what was "choice worthy" and therefore was

> neither capable nor in need of a justification of its desirability from the standpoint of its purposiveness . . . In the end, this is the birth of the concept of reason: the more what is desirable is displayed for all in a way that is convincing to all, the more those involved discover themselves in this common reality; and to that extent human beings possess freedom in the positive sense, they have their true identity in that common reality (Gadamer, 1976–1981, p. 77).

Thus, to the question, "Where do we have such a transparency in the communal character of the ways of life in our society?" (pp. 77–78), Gadamer answers, in theory which articulates the moral sense of practice.

Practical Philosophy

Gadamer develops a theory of practice based on preference or prior choice by interpreting Aristotle's conception of practical philosophy. He follows his general approach to the interpretation of philosophical texts which has been succinctly described by Donald Polkinghorne (1983) as "a dialectical interaction between the expectations of the interpreter and the meanings in the text" (p.226). Gadamer's expectation in interpreting Aristotle's practical wisdom is set forth as a question: What is practice? (Gadamer, pp. 45–46, 69). We are concerned with his understanding of that question, not with the issue, raised by some scholars, of whether Gadamer's approach leads to an adequate interpretation of Aristotle (Hoy, 1978, pp. 103–117 and Polkinghorne, 1983, pp. 228–233). Our purpose is to seek a more adequate understanding of nursing through interpreting Gadamer's philosophy of practice, much as he seeks understanding of practice through interpretation of Aristotle's practical wisdom. In pursuing this purpose, we will approach Gadamer's philosophy of practice with the question: What is nursing?

According to Gadamer, practice in its broadest sense "stands between activity and situatedness" and can refer to all living beings. But what makes practice specifically human is *"prohairesis*, which . . . means 'preference' and 'prior choice.'" Human practice exists in the "eminent sense of the word" when a free citizen makes a decision and that "decision takes its bearings by the order of preferences guiding one's life conduct, whether it be pleasure, power and honor, or knowledge" (Gadamer, 1976–1981, pp. 90–91). For Gadamer practical knowledge involves knowing what to prefer among human values and how to choose that preference actively as an individual in community.

Gadamer, drawing on Aristotle, makes an important distinction between practical knowledge and *techne*.

> And so practical philosophy is determined by the line drawn between the practical knowledge of the person who chooses freely and the acquired skill of the expert that Aristotle named *techne*. Practical philosophy, then has to do not with the learnable crafts and skills, however essential this dimension of human ability too is for the communal life of humanity. Rather it has to do with what is each individual's due as a citizen and what constitutes his *arete* or excellence. Hence, practical philosophy needs to raise to the level of reflective awareness the distinctively human trait of having *prohairesis* (Gadamer, 1976–1981, p. 92).

Regardless of whether this human trait concerns being oriented toward preferring the excellent or being prudent "in deliberating and taking counsel" in "guiding action," the preference or the deliberation has to be guided by its "relationship to the good" (Gadamer, 1976–1981, p. 92).

Not only can practical knowledge not be reduced to *techne* because it is primarily concerned with the good, but because practical knowledge "gives direction to action" which is "called for by concrete situations in which we choose the thing to be done." Since "no learned and mastered technique can spare us the task of deliberation and decision," practical knowledge is not "expert know-how in the sense of a knowledgeable mastery of operational procedures (*poiesis*)." Instead it is "a unique sort of science" which "must arise from practice itself and, with all the typical generalizations that it brings to explicit consciousness, be related back to practice" (Gadamer, 1976–1981, p. 92).

As an example of Gadamer's treatment of practical wisdom, consider the perennial problem for nurses of having enough time to relate personally to their patients. Some nurses, following the contemporary American preference for technology, which comes from the Greek word, "*techne*," could seek more time in one of two ways. Some nurses seek more efficient use of time through improved methods or techniques for doing their routine work. Other nurses search for a theory which orders their working regime efficiently. But nurses who possess practical wisdom would examine the priorities in nursing and make decisions about the use of time on the basis of that which is choice-worthy. The latter, even though they might not articulate it in this way, would be ordering their day by moral priorities in accordance with what is good for the patient. And this moral decision-making would not originate from outside of practice but choices would be made on the basis of the good at which nursing practice aims. Thus practical wisdom, rather than new methodology, scientific theory or technology, would improve nursing practice.

Unfortunately, Gadamer gives only cursory treatment of how a practice is learned. He does say that learning a practice "demands of the one learning it the same indissoluble relationship to practice it does of the one teaching it" (Gadamer, 1976–1981, p. 93). But for some reason he fails to develop the implications of Aristotle's treatment of practical wisdom for learning a practice. Aristotle contended that practical wisdom could be learned only through experience. It cannot be learned by the immature and the inexperienced as mathematics can. Practical wisdom is acquired by engaging in activity from which the universal is grasped from particular experiences (1142a: 14–20 All quotes from W. D. Ross translation). Thus it cannot be taught as theory detached from experience to be applied to later action. Instead practical wisdom is acquired by experience, i.e., doing good acts. Thus, the practice of nursing would be learned through experience rather than by applying theory to practice. In fact, one way in which one could recognize a practice would be that it is primarily learned through experience. The fact that nursing has been and is taught by having novices engage in practice implies that nursing is indeed a practice.

Aristotle's treatment of how one learns to be morally good through practical wisdom also has important implications for nursing. For Aristotle practical wisdom aims at good action which "is itself an end" (1140b: 7). Good action is an end because in it universal human good and the particular are one. In addition, we engage in practical wisdom "not in order to know what virtue is but in order to become good" (1103b: 27–28).

> It is well said, then, that it is by doing just acts that the just man is produced, and by doing temperate acts the temperate man; without doing these no one would have even a prospect of becoming good.
>
> But most people do not do these, but take refuge in theory and think they are being philosophers and will become good in this way, behaving somewhat like patients who listen attentively to their doctors, but do none of the things they are ordered to do. As the latter will not be made well in body by such a course of treatment, the former will not be made well in soul by such a course in philosophy (1105b: 9–18).

Obviously, the reason for teaching nursing ethics to nurses is not primarily to give them knowledge of ethics but to make them morally good nurses. This can not be accomplished by teaching them to apply philosophical ethical theories to the moral problems they encounter in nursing practice. Instead it requires that nursing ethics be taught clinically, because, as Aristotle says, if we are to "become good . . . we must examine the nature of our actions, namely how we ought to do them" (1103b: 29–30).

Since practical wisdom concerns good action, which is an end in itself, it differs from expert knowledge of technique. Practical philosophy is judged by its ability to recognize and to concretize the good in human life. Thus it differs from productive science which aims at making things through efficient technique and by the quality of the thing made justifies the technique. In our technological society, the idea of method comes from the productive sciences and therefore reduces method to technique. And further, since our productivity often results from scientific discovery, we tend to regard method as applied science. But since practical wisdom selects good actions which are ends in themselves, it can neither be treated as applied science nor can its methods be reduced to technique.

Hermeneutics

Gadamer contends that hermeneutics—the art of understanding through interpretation—can lead to theory of practice.

> As far as hermeneutics is concerned it is quite to the point to confront the separation of theory from practice entailed in the modern notion of the theoretical science and practical-technical application with an idea of knowledge that has taken the opposite path leading from practice toward making it aware of itself theoretically (Gadamer, 1976–1981, p. 131).

Thus, hermeneutics would develop theory by articulating practice in a way which makes practitioners aware of the sense of their practice.

Such theoretical self-awareness would not, according to Gadamer, come from the "neutral specialized knowledge of the expert who enters upon tasks" as "a non-participating observer" (p. 135).

> The virtue of practical reason is not to be thought of as a neutral capacity for finding the practical means for correct purposes or ends, but it is inseparably bound up with what Aristotle calls *ethos*. *Ethos* for him is *arche*, the "that" from which all practical-political enlightenment has to set out (Gadamer, 1976–1981, p. 133).

In other words, Gadamer contends that Aristotle believed that practical philosophy presupposes the normative ideas in which we are raised and which found our social life (*ethos*). Of course, these ideas are not immutable and are transformed over time. The human scientist rather than being a "nonparticipating observer ... endeavors ... to bring to our reflective awareness the communality that binds everyone together" (p. 135).

Hermeneutics for Gadamer (1976–1981) is "devoted to that understanding whose universal theme is humanity embedded within traditions" (p. 136). Thus hermeneutics is "not just a repertory of methods ... but philosophy. It not only accounts for the procedures applied by science but also gives an account of the questions that are prior to the application of every science ..., the questions that are determinative for all human knowing and doing, the greatest of questions, that are decisive for human beings as human and their choice of the good" (p. 137).

Gadamer's hermeneutical philosophy indicates why the philosophy of nursing is needed for students of nursing, both in the sense of neophytes who are learning nursing and veteran practitioners who are attempting to make sense out of their practice. Practical philosophy, as Gadamer interprets it, is not the detached examination of the true, good, and beautiful which often serves as a caricature of philosophy for those who are serious practitioners engaged in realizing concrete good in the world. Instead, practical philosophy is an interpretation of how that concrete good is embodied in practice. This interpretation, not only articulates the essence of practice as embodied ways of seeking that good, but criticizes it and seeks the possibilities for improvement inherent in it. Gadamer also directs us to a dimension of health care practice which is often overlooked by our society with its stress on the supposed neutrality of science and technology. In nursing this stress often leads to the unwarranted conclusion that nursing should consist of scientifically established truths which, when applied to nursing care as technique, will achieve experimentally-determined results. Those who hold this view consider values as private visions of the good. Since morality, for them, concerns private visions of the good, professional ethics is merely a concensus reached by individual practitioners. But, according to Gadamer, this dichotomy between values and practice is nonsense. Society, itself, is constituted by fundamental values which are embedded in its cultural ways of being. These cultural ways are in turn embodied in the practice which fosters the goods of society. The art of interpretation articulates, criticizes, and improves these practices in terms of the goods they seek. The practice of health care consists of traditional ways of fostering the psychological and physical well-being of persons, especially those who are ill. In the following chapters, we will show how this good is embedded in the practice of nursing. Our immediate purpose in this chapter, however, is to describe how virtue is related to practice and how practice, rather than being static, is improved through realizing its inherent possibilities, not only in changing its ways for pursuing the good but also by new visions of what constitutes the good of the practice.

MacIntyre on Practice and Virtue

MacIntyre (1984) further develops Gadamer's contention that practice is aimed at moral good by showing how practice and virtue are integrally related to each other. He contends that a particular practice provides "the arena in which the virtues are exhibited and in terms of which they are to receive their primary, if incomplete, definition"

(p. 187). Although he does not limit his treatment of virtue to practice, we will focus on his treatment of the relationship of virtue to practice and suggest its implications for nursing. MacIntyre does not define the word practice in complete agreement with current everyday usage as the following definition will make evident.

> By a 'practice' I am going to mean any coherent and complex form of socially established cooperative human activity through which goods internal to that form of activity are realized in the course of trying to achieve those standards of excellence which are appropriate to, and partially definitive of, that form of activity, with the result that human powers to achieve excellence, and human conceptions of the ends and good involved, are systematically extended (p. 187).

His definition regards practices as whole systems and not individual skills. For example, "bricklaying is not a practice; architecture is. Planting turnips is not a practice; farming is" (p. 187). He regards specific scientific inquiries like physics, chemistry and biology, researching and writing history and painting as examples of practices. Not only are the arts and sciences practices, but politics, in the ancient sense of making and sustaining communal life, is a practice. Obviously, his definition of practice would include both medicine and nursing. One essential key to understanding MacIntyre's conception of practice is "the notion of goods internal to a practice" (p. 188). Negatively, this means that one can not engage in a practice for external rewards. Instead, one engages in a practice for the goods inherent in that practice. These internal goods can only be specified in terms of the actual practice and through examples from that practice and "they can only be identified and recognized by the experience of participating in the practice in question" (pp. 188–189). Further, the excellences of practice can only be understood historically as part of a tradition. These excellences are judged in terms of what the practice produces as a whole. For example, in art this includes not only the excellence of the paintings produced but also the skill developed

by the artist in painting them and the quality of life he lives
as artist.

Practices not only involve achievement of goods but require "standards of excellence and obedience to rules as
well" (p. 190). One enters a practice by accepting the authority of the standards and judging performance by them.
These standards are not only gifts from the past to novice
practitioners but "their achievement is a good for the whole
community who participate in the practice" (p. 190). Thus,
MacIntyre defines virtue as

> *an acquired human quality the possession and exercise of*
> *which tends to enable us to achieve those goods which*
> *are internal to practices and the lack of which effectively*
> *prevents us from achieving any such goods (p. 191)*

According to MacIntyre, recognizing virtues within
practices requires making two necessary contrasts. The first
is between practice and a "set of technical skills" (p. 193).
What

> is distinctive in a practice is in part the way in which con-
> ceptions of the relevant goods and ends which the techni-
> cal skills serve—and every practice does require the exer-
> cise of technical skills—are transformed and enriched by
> these extensions of human powers and by that regard for
> its own internal goods which are partially definitive of
> each particular practice or type of practice (p. 193).

Thus practices do not have fixed goals. Instead, goals are
"transmuted by the history of the activity" (p. 194). Thus,
the history of a practice is more than recounting of the improvement in the technical skills since it primarily recounts the relationship of virtue to practice. Further, those
who enter the practice not only are related to their contemporary practitioners but also to those who preceded them in
their practice and brought it to its present state.

The second contrast is between internal goods of the
practice and the external goods of the institutions which
support practice. Not only are practitioners related to the

history of the practice but also to the institutions which support practice, in the case of nursing, hospitals, nursing homes, and clinics. These institutions are concerned with what MacIntyre calls external goods in that they supply the wealth, material goods, structured power and status necessary to support and foster continued practice. Since the institution focuses on external goods, there is apt to be tension between it and practitioners who focus on internal goods. In an age such as ours which values external goods over internal goods, there is always the threat that the institution will lose sight of the fact that its primary function is to foster the practice.

Obviously, MacIntyre is not an institutionalist, but is he a traditionalist? He is a traditionalist only in the sense that his position would commit nurses to begin with their own practice and its internal goods rather than with theories and models external to the practice of nursing. He is not a traditionalist if that means that one desires to preserve practice as it has been in the past. In fact, he contends that a practice which attempts to remain static is dead. He advocates change through realization of the possibilities inherent in present practice, including the goods which are inherent in it and constitutive of it.

> So when an institution—a university, say, or a farm, or a hospital—is the bearer of a tradition of practice or practices, its common life will be partly, but in a centrally important way, constituted by a continuous argument as to what a university is and ought to be or what good farming is or what good medicine is. Traditions, when vital, embody continuities of conflict. Indeed when a tradition becomes Burkean, it is always dying or dead (MacIntyre, 1984, p. 222).

In contrast to a dead tradition, a living tradition is a "historically extended, socially embodied argument . . . about the goods which constitute that tradition" (p. 222). An individual's search for his or her own good is always a part of the traditional argument of his or her time. Thus, practitioners work in a practice embedded in and "made intelligible in terms of the larger and longer history of the tradition through which the practice in its present form was conveyed to" them (p. 222). Whether a practice remains a living one or dies depends on "the exercise or lack of exercise of relevant virtues!" (p. 223). But these virtues are relevant not only to the good internal to practices but also to the good of individual lives as a whole. Practices also must contribute to the good of the total historic community from whose traditions they derive their lives and of which "they are contemporary embodiments" (p. 223). But continuing these traditions does not mean retaining the status quo. In fact, it "is rather the case that an adequate sense of tradition manifests itself in a grasp of those future possibilities which the past has made available to the present" (p. 223).

In contrast to MacIntyre's beliefs that practices should be transformed from realizing the possibilities from within the historic tradition, many advocated reforms in nursing come from theories and models external to the practice of nursing. For this reason, Benner's (1984) attempt to find excellence in nursing from within nursing practice is both novel and refreshing. But she treats nursing excellence in terms of competencies to be achieved rather than in terms of virtue. In seeking excellence in nursing practice through exemplars, Benner is challenging those moderns for whom "the concept of a practice with goods internal to itself" has been "removed to the margins of our lives" (MacIntyre, 1918, p. 227). But she sides with modernity in choosing to treat excellence in nursing in terms of competencies rather than virtues. However, if MacIntyre's treatment of the relationship of practice to virtue is right, one should be able to find virtues as well as competencies in the examples of excellence given by Benner. Benner, in fact, points us in this direction because she treats competencies, not in the usual sense of skills to be learned but rather, as instantiations of excellence as practiced by exemplars (Benner, personal communication, July 1987).

Actually Benner's organization of the competencies under seven domains provides the key for understanding the competencies in terms of virtues. For example, the first two domains are the helping role and the teaching-coaching function. Treating the helping function as a virtue would better articulate Benner's surprise concerning help-giving by nurses.

> Nevertheless, I found myself frankly surprised at the quality of caring I observed. In an individualistic age where power, status, and control are taken for granted as the basic motivating forces in human interactions, I was prepared to observe power plays; instead, I found nurses who were skilled in avoiding power play with their patients (Benner, 1984, p. 48).

Not only did she find that nurses put help-giving above power, status, and control, but they also treated patients as persons to be helped rather than problems to be solved. Rather than imposing the instrumentalist language of nursing technology on patients, nurses entered into the meanings the patients gave to their situation. Thus, their helpfulness went beyond "narrow definitions of 'therapeutic,'" to help patients transform the meaning of their illness and situation and, when circumstances warranted, they simply had "the courage to be with the patient, offering whatever comfort the situation allows" (p. 49). This movement beyond narrow professional expectations and technological conceptions to empathetic understanding and sensitive contextual care can be articulated as the virtue of helpfulness as well as the competency of fulfilling the function of the helping role.

The virtue of helpfulness should be balanced with the virtue of independence. When this is done, self-care would be focal to Benner's second domain, the teaching-coaching function. In Heidegger's (1962, pp. 159–160) interpretation, caring goes beyond helping others by teaching others to care for themselves. Nurses, beginning with what is "foreign and fearful to the patient," (Benner, 1984, p. 77) help patients interpret the meaning of their illness and what they experience in treatment and recovery. In addition to preparing them for treatment and recovery, they teach them how to care for themselves as recovery permits. True, this aspect of nursing can be described as the teaching-coaching function as Benner does or as a model for a theory of nursing as Orem (1980) does, but our contention is that the virtue of self-care is necessary to balance the traditional virtue of helpfulness.

In treating the domains as functions, Benner emphasizes the doing aspect of nursing practice. When practice is understood in terms of virtues, the being aspect of practice is stressed. For example, three of Benner's (1984) domains, diagnosis and patient monitoring; effective management of rapidly changing situations; and administering and monitoring therapeutic interventions and regimens, (p. 46) all stress what the nurse does. But what must she *be* in order to carry out these functions? Certainly, she must be resolute and flexible possessing that delicate balance between fortitude and flexibility exemplified by Florence Nightingale (Woodham-Smith, 1983).

Another delicate balance of virtue required in the practice of nursing is evident in Benner's domains of monitoring and ensuring the quality of health care practices and of organizational and work-role competencies. These domains require the virtue of loyalty which maintains the system of health care. But such system maintenance must be balanced by the demand for just reform of that system so that it provides higher quality and more equal and fair distribution of services.

In line with MacIntyre's contention that living practices not only change techniques and structure but also virtues, it is interesting that in Benner's treatment of the domains we see such a shift in virtues. Nursing, traditionally, valued the virtues of helpfulness, fortitude, and loyalty. In contemporary nursing, helpfulness is balanced by fostering self-help and independence. We see a similar shift from the traditional virtue of fortitude to openness. Traditionally, more stress was placed on fortitude in nursing because nurses operated within systems fixed by others to which nurses had to accommodate themselves. But now with more flexibility in health care institutions and with changes unrelated to institutional policies, such as women's liberation, nurses increasingly have acquired the virtue of flexibility in the balance with the traditional virtue of fortitude. In the past, the virtue of loyalty to the institution or system was a cardinal virtue to the nurse. Now, the virtue which is required to balance loyalty is the virtue of justice.

Our purpose is not to list all the virtues of nursing in general or even all those suggested by Benner's competencies. Instead, we merely want to illustrate that the virtues of nursing are inherent in nursing practice by showing that competencies drawn from nursing can be readily translated into virtues. When they are understood in this way, being and doing are integrally related in a communal practice with an inherent moral sense.

Chapter 6

The Moral Sense in Nursing Practice

If Gadamer's and MacIntyre's treatment of practice is sound, then the primary sense of nursing practice should be a moral sense. Is this true? If it is, why is the moral sense emphasized so seldom in the nursing literature?

Certainly, the moral sense was the primary sense of nursing as Florence Nightingale envisioned it. Florence Nightingale founded nursing upon the moral sense of practice. In fact, according to Rosenberg, Florence Nightingale viewed the hospital as a moral universe. For Nightingale, nursing practice was fundamentally moral rather than scientific, as Rosenberg makes very clear.

> Nightingale saw the nurse's role as both multifaceted and indispensable. It was also fundamentally moral. Nightingale explicitly contended that a trained nurse's endowments must be ultimately spiritual; the technical abilities which she might acquire were, if not precisely subordinate to her moral powers, at least subsequent to and dependent upon them. Not the least of these moral qualities was—and here Nightingale obviously made a personal plea—activism itself. As she put it, "patience and resignation" in a nurse "are but other words for carelessness or indifference—contemptible, if in regard to herself; culpable, if in regard to her sick" (pp. 125–126).

Excerpts fom "The Moral Sense and Health Care" by Scudder and Bishop, in *The Moral Sense in the Communal Significance of Life, Analecta Husserliana 20* [edited by] A-T Tymieniecka, pp. 125–158, copyright 1986 by D. Reidel Publishing Co. Used by permission.

Nursing and medicine for Nightingale were concerned primarily with care rather than cure. She made this very clear in her *Notes on Nursing*.

> Pathology teaches the harm that disease has done. But it teaches nothing more . . . It is often thought that medicine is the curative process. It is no such thing; medicine is the surgery of functions, as surgery proper is that of limbs and organs. Neither can do anything but remove obstructions; neither can cure; nature alone cures. Surgery removes the bullet out of the limb, which is an obstruction to cure, but nature heals the wound (Nightingale, 1859–1946, p. 74).

As Rosenberg (1979) points out:

> All nursing could accomplish—and it was no small achievement—was to put the patient into the best possible condition for nature to effect its plan of cure. But although a hospital could not *cure*, it seemed self-evident to Nightingale that it could and must avert the spread of infection and more generally promote the body's internally direct efforts to regain health (p. 126).

Nursing set the right conditions for healing by maintaining the proper environment and social order in the hospital. This meant that hospitals must have proper ventilation, must be clean, serve proper food, and keep the patients clean. Thus, Nightingale rightly saw a close relationship between health, behavior, and social environment. That she did not adopt the germ theory on contagion is not surprising, in that, it was not accepted by many physicians and medical scientists in her time. In fact, as Rosenberg points out, John Snow, who is responsible for demonstrating that cholera was a water-born disease, had a view of disease much like that of Nightingale. Yet his discovery did much to eliminate the threat of cholera in Europe. In a similar fashion, Nightingale's stress on "a more humane hospital environment—toward better sanitation, adequate ventilation, improved diet, competent nursing," (Rosenberg, 1979, p. 130) did greatly improve patient care even though she rejected the germ theory of disease which would have accounted for the success of the nursing practices she advocated. Ironically, Nightingale did use the science of statistics to show that the hospital reforms she advocated were effective in promoting healing and good health. Thus, although she did not adequately understand the scientific side of medicine, she did, in fact, understand good practice and health care. More importantly, she understood that establishing good care practices and actual good care by particular nurses rested on a moral foundation.

What has happened to nursing practice to diminish the moral foundation which Nightingale envisioned? Actually, as we shall show, the moral foundation is very much evident in practice. However, nursing educators and theorists have taught nurses to articulate their profession in terms drawn from theories outside nursing practice. Since these theories are usually scientific or pseudo-scientific, they, unlike nursing practice, do not have a moral foundation and indeed follow the pattern which Gadamer contended leads to the degeneration of practice into technique.

Interestingly, Benner's attempt to disclose nursing excellence from examination of actual practice, both explicitly and implicitly, shows the moral sense, even though she articulates that excellence in terms of competencies. This is not surprising since, as we have shown following MacIntyre, the competencies she lists can easily be translated into moral virtues. However, Benner and her team did find surprising the degree to which the helpful attitude of nurses was evident in actual practice. This suggests that when nurses are engaged in practice, nursing may indeed have a moral foundation even though practitioners do not articulate the moral sense.

Practices and social institutions can be articulated so that both the professional sense and the moral sense can be disclosed, according to Anna-Teresa Tymieniecka (1983). In fact, she contends that the purposes of the human sciences are to make both articulations. She uses psychiatry as an example. In psychiatry the first sense consists of "capturing, describing, diagnosing and devising therapeutic approaches" to mental illness (Tymieniecka, 1983, p. 41). In the second sense, psychiatry is articulated as "the investigation of the life significance of the moral sense as the foundation of intersubjectivity" and, hence, of psychiatry (Tymieniecka, 1983, p. 42). For Tymieniecka, these articulations are not of two separate phenomena but are different ways of articulating the same phenomena. These two senses of psychiatry are evident in all forms of health care. Health care can be articulated professionally in terms of a concrete practice, such as assessing, monitoring, and intervening, etc. But it also can be articulated in terms of the moral sense in that such care is articulated as concrete benevolence. The moral sense places the good of the other over our own but also allows us to understand "the 'good' of the Other," as "our own good, or the Good in general" (Tymieniecka, 1983, p. 26).

Nurses and Fulfillment in Health Care

Fulfillment comes to nurses, and presumably to other health professionals, when these two senses of care converge so that articulation of the professional sense of practice discloses the moral sense. Interestingly, Huston Smith (1965) has pointed out that "meaning" itself has these two essential meanings: one referring to the intelligibility of an activity and the other to the moral worth of that activity. In nursing and other health care professions, we shall designate these senses as the professional sense and the moral sense. We will show that nurses find fulfillment, as Tymieniecka suggests, when the professional sense and the moral sense become one.

Before the professionalization of nursing, the two senses of nursing were clearly in harmony. For example, on a nursing poster under the painting, "The Sick Child," by Gabriel Metsu, a caption reads, "Nursing: The Oldest Art." Regardless of the accuracy of the claim of "oldest art," it is evident from the painting that caring for the ill is a fundamental human phenomena in which the art of care and the moral sense are conjoined in a personal relationship.

Nursing as a profession was originally merely an extension of personal, direct care for the ill. Historically, nursing has been distinguished by being that health care profession most concerned with direct care. That is, nurses have been assumed to act out of compassion for the ill by doing those things which the ill cannot do for themselves, such as bathing, feeding, and other activities of daily living. But with the advance of medical science and technology since World War II, the function of nurses has been distinguished from that of physicians by contending that nurses care and physicians cure. The stress on cure has led nurses, in addition to direct care, to become the physician's assistant in curing.

When we apply Pellegrino's four senses of medical care to nursing, it becomes evident that one problem in contemporary nursing is to see the relationship between care for the ill in the moral sense and in the professional sense. His first sense of care, personal moral care, is obviously care in the moral sense of caring for an ill person out of compassion. His second sense, direct care—doing for an ill person what they cannot do for themselves—can readily be a concrete expression of the first sense since it requires direct contact between persons. The third and fourth senses of care are obviously professional, and for our purposes, can be considered together as professional care. When combined, professional care includes professional understanding and skill and craftsmanship in the art of actually employing this knowledge and skill in eliminating or alleviating the patient's problem. The advancement of professional knowledge and skill and the advances in medical science and technology *all* have led nurses to stress professional cure at the expense of the personal moral and direct senses of care. However, the logic of Pellegrino's treatment of care in medicine clearly assigns the priority to the personal moral sense of care over professional and direct care but incorporates them within it. If this is true for medicine even with its current stress on cure, it certainly should be true for nursing with its traditional focus on care. The findings of a study we conducted concerning fulfillment in nurses, as well as a followup study, certainly supports the contention that both the professional sense and the direct sense of care are incorporated within the moral sense of personal care in actual nursing practice.

Investigation

Our initial investigation attempted to discover whether practicing nurses regarded nursing as direct, personal care out of compassion or performance of professional roles aimed at cure utilizing medical science and technology. Also, we attempted to discover how nurses understood the relationship of caring as personal and direct care to professional knowledge and craftsmanship. We especially wanted to know whether the stress on medical science and technology had led nursing away from traditional care given out of compassion.

We knew that we would encounter at least two difficulties in attempting to elicit the meaning of care from the direct experience of nurses. In previous attempts to arrive at the sense of professional care from personal experiences of nurses (Bishop) and of teachers (Scudder), we had encountered two pitfalls. First, when asked to treat their experience by descriptive methods, some teachers and nurses merely describe what they typically do. Second, some nurses and teachers who had learned in theory classes that good practice includes x, y and z, merely determine whether x, y and z were actually done in their practice.

To avoid these pitfalls, we selected a phenomenological procedure advocated by Barritt, Beekman, Bleeker, and Muldering (1983). We asked sixty practicing nurses and senior nursing students to respond to the following:

I. Write an account of a single experience, something simple and straightforward from your nursing practice, when you felt most fulfilled as a nurse and thought you were most completely being a nurse. As much as possible stick to a descriptive language and do not include interpretations and attributions of causality to your writing. Don't lose yourself in factual details. It all begins with the lived experience and that is what you should strive to describe.

II. Write an account of a single experience, something simple and straighforward from your nursing practice, when you felt least fulfilled as a nurse and thought you were least being a nurse. As much as possible stick to a descriptive language and do not include interpretations and attributions of causality to your writing. Don't lose yourself in factual details. It all begins with the lived experience and that is what you should strive to describe.

We asked for these concrete descriptions of actual experience in order to avoid generalized descriptions of routine behavior or evaluation of professional activity in terms of theoretically derived criteria. We reasoned that in telling of a concrete experience in which the nurses felt that they had been most clearly and completely a nurse or least fully a nurse, we could arrive at the experiential meaning of care for nurses.

Most Fulfilling Experiences

The responses of these nurses made evident that their most fulfilling experiences were those in which care was experienced as personal moral care which subsumed professional care and/or direct care. All of their descriptions focused on personal caring relationships with patients, regardless of whether they involved either direct care and/or care which required a high degree of professional knowledge and skill and professional language. The following description illustrates the point:

> Approximately 25 years ago I was assigned to work with a female patient who had suffered third degree burns over 60% of her body. I was assigned to her every working day for approximately one year. She required intensive nursing care as well as psychological support. Initially, she was on complete isolation. Her care was time-consuming and

challenging. She was on a Stryker Frame, receiving intravenous fluids, had dressings over 60% of her body, and
was completely dependent for all physical needs. I spent
an average of three to four hours per day carrying out the
doctor's orders as well as providing essential nursing care.
We came to know each other as I have never known
another patient. She trusted me and talked of her husband's alcoholism, her concern for the welfare and safety
of three small children, financial worries and her physical
pain and depression. She needed several operations for
skin grafting, intensive rehabilitative services and the
emotional support from nursing staff to cope. It was such
a pleasure to be a part of the healing process and to see
her leave the hospital after a year's hospitalization, even
though emotionally a part of me went home with her.

In the above case, in which care is present in all senses,
it is evident that the sense of fulfillment came from personal moral care, i.e., a personal relationship in which professional activities are done out of compassion. Fulfillment
from these professional activities seems to bear little or no
relationship to whether caring was done as direct care or
professional care. One nurse who responded put this very
well concerning direct care in the following description:

I felt most fulfilled as a nurse when one day a patient at
my place of employment told me, "Things are just not
right when you are not here." I had been giving her bedside care, medication, treatments, and conversation. I
oriented her to date and time, the events going on in the
world. This statement made me feel I had accomplished
more than "just nursing."

Note that in the above description "just nursing" refers to
caring as direct care. She seems to be making a distinction
between that which can be learned as a practice and that
which is uniquely a part of her personality and of her relationship with this person, her patient. However, "just
nursing" does not imply that practice should be separated
from personal relationships, but that fulfillment as a nurse

requires that the practice be encompassed in personal care for the ill person.

Personal care also encompassed professional care, as is evident in the following description in which compassion is expressed almost entirely as professional care.

> My most fulfilling experience deals with my first and only cord prolapse of a woman progressing with the aid of Pitocin stimulation and how a normally progressing labor can suddenly change into a critical episode of life-saving measures for her unborn child. What made this experience memorable was the fact that I detected what felt like a cord at a vaginal check and the physician was called, but misdiagnosed his vaginal check. My suspicions called for another check and fetal heart monitoring. Without further doubt of what was occurring, the physician was recalled and an emergency C-Section took place with a healthy baby boy born. It took place quickly but was particularly self-satisfying—especially since I see the child and his Mom and Dad upon occasion and see his growth and progress.

Even when all the senses of care are well integrated, fulfillment for the nurses came from the moral sense becoming apparent in the professional sense as in the following example.

> Two years ago I had the oppportunity to deliver total patient care to a 25-year-old girl with end stage congestive cardiomyopathy. She was in congestive heart failure with many ventricular life threatening arrhythmias. She was well aware of the fact that she was going to die and admitted her fright to me and also asked me point blank if she was going to die. We were able to discuss such problems as how could this be explained to her 7-year-old daughter? Who would care for her 7-year-old daughter and her own 16-year-old retarded sister? I also discussed with her family, some of the fears she had acknowledged and encouraged them to discuss these things with her. Her main request to me was that I sit by her bed during the night and

simply hold her hand. In addition to ministering to these needs, I also monitored her vital signs, changes in physical assessment, titrated various vasopressors and vasodilators to maintain optimum cardiac output. I overrode our strict visiting policies to allow her husband and daughter to sit at her bedside as they wished with the understanding that they would promptly leave if asked to do so by any of us. This patient remained in my unit for 4–5 weeks in critical condition before dying and though we all felt the hurt of losing her, we also felt the joy obtained by providing emotional and physical support along with patient teaching to both patient and family and helped both patient and family to accept and begin to deal with her inevitable death.

In the above example, the direct and professional senses of care are well integrated into benevolent care which brought fulfillment to the nurse. Also in the above case, as in the other cases, this care goes beyond the immediate clinical situation to include family, orientation to the outside world, and/or continued relationship after the illness.

In the nurses' descriptions of their most fulfilling experiences, the stress was on the nurse-patient relationship rather than profession-nurse relationship, the hospital-nurse relationship or the physician-nurse relationship. Even in the few descriptions which included cooperation between nurse and physician, the fulfillment came not from the good nurse-physician relationship but from the better care for the patient which resulted from their cooperation.

Least Fulfilling Experiences

Although the least fulfilling experiences were varied, the majority of the factors causing concern were those inhibiting patient care. The most frequently cited inhibiting factor was uncooperative patients. Other factors were patient overloads, lack of skill or knowledge, and lack of contact or cooperation with physicians. For example, one nurse stated, "I felt least like a nurse when I had twelve patients and only enough time to change the beds and bathe the patients" and another nurse wrote "I felt least fulfilled when an elderly man wanted me to talk with him and I had too many beds to make, too many baths to give." Another nurse wrote that her least fulfilling experience was her unsuccessful attempts to locate the physician of a patient experiencing chest pain. Time lapsed and the patient died. The nurse expressed feelings of inadequacy, helplessness, and sadness.

Some of the unfulfilling experiences *seemed* not to focus on patient care, however. For instance, some nurses resent physicians not respecting their professional judgment.

> I was never allowed to use my nursing judgment and I had to perform every task strictly by the rules or by doctor's orders. The time when I did attempt to make a judgment and communicate that to others, I was generally made to feel that I had made an error or I was disciplined verbally that it was not my place to make these kinds of decisions.

Others resent doing maid-type activities, especially when patients treat them as servants. "I felt unfulfilled when I had a patient who treated me as a maid instead of a nurse. She constantly was ordering me around asking me to empty her trash can and clean up her room" and the "patient requested services of me that were more like a housekeeper." Nursing students especially resented rigid cold supervisors. One resented a patient's flirtations. "The patient made many 'flirty' comments which I ignored. 'My you're a pretty little thing.' 'If I had you, I sure would treat you like a princess.' I pretended not to be fazed by his behavior, but caring for this type of patient was definitely not fulfilling." Although the above resentment of affronts to personal dignity and to professional judgment and status seem not to inhibit care in the moral sense, actually it does. As Tymieniecka (1983, p. 35) points out, one's benevolent care of another needs to be recognized and appreciated by the other. In all of the above cases not only was that recognition and appreciation not given, but the response made such care difficult.

The problem of how to relate to dying patients was often mentioned. Some nurses found that they were able to develop an intense personal relationship with dying patients. They were able to discuss aspects of living and dying for the first time. Patients and families were very appreciative. In two cases, the dying patients through their personal relationships with nursing students contributed to the students' confidence in themselves as nurses and as caring persons. "As a nursing student I was assigned to a dying patient. In the midst of all her pain and suffering, she constantly praised everything I did for her. Just to experience the presence of a person so at peace with herself was a terrific highlight in my life." In contrast, some nurses found caring for dying patients least fulfilling because they were unable to help them and as a consequence felt hopelessness and depression. "When I had my first experience with a dying patient, who had throat cancer, I watched this patient slowly suffocate and I felt utterly useless." Another patient "had no family and was a hemiplegic due to multiple trauma. He could only communicate with notewriting and he scribbled a note, 'Please let me die.' I felt inadequate and confused."

One surprising finding from examining these descriptions was that the response of the patient to the nurse's professional and personal care was the most important ingredient in determining whether or not an experience was fulfilling or unfulfilling. We had expected that nurses would find relationships with physicians and hospital bureaucratic requirements least fulfilling. But hostile and uncooperative patients contributed most often to lack of fulfillment. "I felt least fulfilled when the 13-year-old boy's first words were cussing at us, to leave him alone. How dare he! We had saved his life." In contrast appreciative, supportive, and cooperative patients contributed most to fulfillment. "I felt most fulfilled while caring for a forty-three-year old woman with metastatic cancer. We cried together, laughed together, and conspired together to meet her needs even if it meant bending hospital policy."

Our conclusion from this exploratory investigation is that nurses feel most fulfilled when they experience their professional care as personal benevolent caring for the ill. The way of caring for the ill, whether it was in the sense of direct care or professional care, did not seem to be essential. The nurses seemed most fulfilled when direct or professional care was done out of the moral sense and in a personal relationship with ill persons who appreciated and confirmed the moral worth of their care.

The conclusion of our initial study has been confirmed by a follow-up study, which included twenty practicing nurses from a large university medical center. We chose a medical center because nurses who work in these centers usually work with patients who are critically ill and use a higher level of technology in that care. Even with the greater stress on technology and professional skill, nineteen of the twenty nurses clearly supported our previous findings that nurses feel more fulfilled when the moral and personal sense of their work is dominant. In the only exception, a follow-up interview indicated that this particular nurse found fulfillment in both the moral sense and technical expertise but when asked to make a choice between the two, she decided that she usually found more fulfillment from exercising technical expertise than from recognizing the good in which that expertise eventuated.

The overwhelming affirmation of the moral sense in nursing practice surprised us rather than the one exception. From the literature treating trends in nursing, we originally expected to find a real struggle in nursing practice between those who believe professional and technical expertise to be the essence of nursing and those who thought that a moral and personal caring relationship with patients was its essence. We were amazed at the way in which professional and technical expertise was incorporated into the moral sense. One nurse described a patient who had undergone an aneurysm clipping, as "a GCS5T, E4, M1, VT, [who] opened his eyes but [had] no movement and was trached." Obviously, to understand the sense of this illness and treatment, one needs technical-professional knowledge. But one needs no such knowledge to understand the sense of meaning within which the nurse incorporated the technical description. She concluded this description as follows: "I can't describe the sensation I felt; but to see him follow a command for the first time—moving his thumb made me feel wonderful inside. All of our diligent nursing care, positioning, ROM, stimulation, etc. was working and it felt good." Interestingly, in a follow-up interview with this nurse, she stated that although this work was very technical, she would not remain in nursing if it were not for personal and moral fulfillment.

Routine Practice and Compassion

The nurses in both studies felt fulfilled when the professional sense of care accomplished what its moral sense of care intended and the patients recognized and appreciated the nursing care. But how often does this occur in a nursing career filled with routine roles, a multitude of tasks, nursing care plans and complicated equipment? A cynical nurse might say, "Sure there are exceptionally fulfilling moments but for the most part, nursing is doing the routine tasks of patient care." But such cynicism fails to recognize that professional roles, knowledge and skills are not necessarily separate from or in opposition to compassion and personal involvement. In fact, Ricoeur (1965) shows us why the two are closely related to each other. In an essay Ricoeur contrasts being a neighbor with providing a service. For Ricoeur, one is a neighbor in the first person. The meaning of being a neighbor is being available to another person when you are needed as you are needed. In contrast, a social role is performed in the third person. One performs specific services by virtue of having a certain social status and the service is provided to those in certain catagories. Does this distinction require one to choose between being a neighbor and performing a social service? Ricoeur thinks not. Both being a neighbor and providing a social service are united in having the common intentionality of charity.

Benevolent intentionally is often obscured by the nature of social function and institutional services.

The ultimate meaning of institution is the service which they render to persons. If no one draws profit from them they are useless. But this ultimate meaning remains hidden (Ricoeur, 1965, p. 109).

When intentionality is hidden we often blame social roles and technology for lack of personal meaning in institutions. But Ricoeur warns of the folly of such accusation.

> The theme of the neighbor is primarily an appeal to the awakening of consciousness. It would be absurd to condemn machines, technocracy, administrative apparatus, social security, etc. Technical procedures and, in general, all 'technicity,' have the innocence of the instrument (p. 107).

Although technology and social roles may obscure personal meaning, they do not necessarily oppose it. Personal meaning appears when the neighbor awakens my moral sense of benevolence and I respond with appropriate care for him. If I respond with routine professional care, then I need confirmation in a first person encounter with *this* person who has benefited from *my* professional service. The following description is an excellent example.

> The most fulfilling experience I ever had was when a child I was caring for arrested but was successfully resuscitated. I had written my notice that day—I wanted out of nursing—it was killing me. The baby stopped breathing while we were on the elevator coming back from X-ray. I did mouth-to-mouth on her until we got back to the room and the code team arrived. The baby responded beautifully. Naturally I felt good. But when the mother praised me for "saving" her baby, I tried to tell her that what I did was not so special; anyone can do mouth-to-mouth. "But it was you," she said. "You were there. If you hadn't wanted to be a nurse in the first place and been working that day, I wouldn't have my baby."

Role and Being

When the nurse in the above example says, "What I did was not so special; anyone can do mouth-to-mouth," she means, "Of course I did that; I'm a nurse; any nurse would do the same thing." If she means that as a nurse, she has a certain defined role and she merely carried it out, then it is literally true that any competent nurse could and would have done it. But the mother is not referring to competency and roles but to her *being* a nurse and *being* there and giving care.

A nurse who performs mouth-to-mouth effectively at the appropriate time could be an inauthentic nurse as well as an authentic nurse. The inauthentic nurse merely plays the role of nurse rather than really *being* a nurse. In contrast, the authentic nurse would say in the above circumstances, "I could not have done otherwise because of the kind of person I am," and also anyone who is really a nurse would do the same. Thus, the statement, "I am a nurse," refers to being rather than social role. This does not mean that being a nurse does not involve what a sociologist would call the role of a nurse or what we believe should be designated a practice for reasons which should be evident by now. But a practice can also be "practice," that is, playing at being a nurse by imitating a practice. For one to authentically be a nurse, a practice has to become a part of his/her being in a way which expresses both the general requirements of the practice and one's particular way of being with others through that practice. When nursing students are novices, the practice is somewhat divorced from them—not because they are inauthentic, but because they have not learned how to appropriate the practice in general, much less as a part of their particular way of being. An authentic veteran nurse, on the other hand, has not only made the practice her own but practices innovatively to meet changing situations in ways which often make new contributions to the practice. An inauthentic nurse is one who, although experienced and veteran still follows the roles and rules of the practice like a novice. For example, a patient was cared for by several nurses, two of whom seemed to be playing roles—one a recent graduate from a nursing program and the other a veteran nurse with many decades of experience. When the patient described his nursing care to other nurses familiar with the hospital, they could easily identify the older nurse from the way she practiced, but they could not idenfity the younger nurse. The novice nurse was practicing as most beginning nurses learn to practice, but the veteran nurse had not appropriated the practice in ways peculiar to her way of being and was incapable of flexible and innovative patient care. Obviously, in this example, the veteran nurse was still playing a role but in a rigid and more "efficient" manner than a novice and, thus, was being a nurse inauthentically.

In the case of the nurse in the resuscitation example, it seems obvious that the nurse was *being* a nurse rather than playing a role. If she had merely been playing a role she would not have said, "Nursing is killing me." Instead, she would have given as her reason for quitting, "They expect too much for what they pay" or "My work is so monotonous and boring" or "I get a lot of guff and no respect." An authentic veteran nurse is not playing a role or mastering a practice but is *being* a nurse through a mastered and personalized practice.

When I am a nurse through particularizing the practice of nursing, then nursing is personal because I express my way of being through it. But personal also can refer to my relationship with the person for whom I am caring. When nursing is personal in this sense, I cease to care for *the* patient and care for Mary Smith, who is my patient.

Nursing becomes personally fulfilling when I personalize the general practice through care for particular persons and have those persons concretely confirm the worth of my being a nurse. The nurse who resuscitated the child, like most nurses, had often carried out her practice assuming that she helped patients but often without much direct evidence or confirmation. Her most fulfilling moment occurred when the personal moral sense of her practice was made manifest to her in a concrete personal relationship through the appreciative response of the mother.

Caring for the ill is generally done by nurses through personalized professional functions and activities. Usually these functions and activities are carried out in faith because there is little direct confirmation of their moral worth. The events and situations which the nurses in our study found fulfilling were those in which they encountered the moral sense of their professional care. Then the meaning of the nursing practice appeared and the moral sense of their vocation as nurse was confirmed. It made little difference whether the neighbor was encountered in direct care or professional care; the moral sense of their profession came from direct encounter with a person for whom they had cared. This deeply felt confirmation of the moral sense of being a nurse occurred when the intentionality of benevolence embedded in the practice of nursing became manifest in a personal relationship in which an ill person was helped. Then the professional sense of being a nurse and the moral sense of being a nurse converged in a practice which integrated personal and professional care.

The Moral Sense in Patients

We have shown that fulfillment in nursing comes from the convergence of the professional sense of practice with its moral sense. When this occurs, professionally established procedures cease to be ends in themselves and become ways of achieving the benevolent goal of nursing. However, for this fulfillment to be achieved, patient and nurse must develop a personal relationship in which patients appreciate and acknowledge their good care. Thus one moral responsibility of patients is to acknowledge good care which confirms the worth of the person giving that care and the practice through which it is given.

The moral sense of health care is usually treated in terms of the physicians' and nurses' relationships and responsibilities to the patient. It is rarely treated in terms of the patient's relationship and moral responsibility to the physician and nurse. Nurses do encourage patients to accept moral responsibility for their own physical and psychological well-being in a general sense. But they rarely think of the patient as a moral being who needs help in articulating and acting from the moral sense of being a patient. Nurses are not alone in this neglect, however. The moral sense of being a patient and of responding to illness and disability is rarely treated in health care literature.

In spite of this neglect, patients often act out of the moral sense in relation to nurses, physicians and other patients. For example, one nursing student in our study gained confidence in her professional ability, a greater sense of her worth as a person, and a greater recognition of the potential for compassion in human beings when an elderly patient dying of cancer responded to her treatment with benevolence. Richard Zaner (1985) was amazed at the degree to which the moral sense pervaded the patient's relationship to physicians and nurses. Zaner points out that patients are unusually patient in their dealings with physicians. They continue to trust physicians even when their treatment indicates that such trust may be unwarranted. Put differently, they tend to give the physicians the benefit of the doubt concerning their treatment. Only when the evidence is overwhelming that they have not been treated adequately or fairly, do most patients confront their physicians. Then they merely expect their physicians to acknowledge their mistakes and not to charge them for inadequate or harmful treatment and to do their best to remedy the hurt and incapacity they have brought about.

> Patients are remarkably resilient and forgiving—published statistics to the contrary notwithstanding. These (and other) patients seem reluctant to pursue legal redress, even where it may not be unreasonable. Unexpectedly, this woman, like so many others, was able to understand that physicians are human, too; that they make mistakes; and that only at times are they culpable. Often, what's important for these patients seems not the mistakes, but the willingness (or unwillingness) of the physician to own up to a mistake and be ready to make amends in some reasonable and caring way (Zaner, 1985, p. 86).

In short, patients expect, as a minimum, fair treatment from their physician.

Patients, however, do want more than fair treatment from their physician. As Zaner (1985) points out, "sick people 'want *to know'*" about their condition (p. 92). The moral sense is evident in the expectation of patients that physicians will honestly apprise them of their condition. That patients seek to understand their condition even when not given adequate information by their physicians amazed physician Robert S. Mendelsohn (1978). He wrote, "a remarkable finding of these interviews is the consistently profound base of information patients manifest about their condition . . . patients are aware of the major aspects as well as the subtleties of causation, diagnosis, treatment alternatives and prediction of outcomes." Mendelsohn admonishes his fellow physicians, "Stop talking down to your patients; stop patronizing them as if they were children or stupid or retarded or all three" (p. viii). Certainly, this implies that patients expect their physicians to have a moral obligation to treat them as adults capable of understanding their condition. Further, they believe that physicians have a moral obligation to help them understand their condition and prospects. Zaner (1985) puts this very well.

> Patients want and seek to know, and in the interest of proper and appropriate dealing with them, the norm that obliges that accurate, adequate, and understandable information be promptly and continuously given to them seems unquestionably demanded (p. 95).

Patients need to know because knowledge of their condition and treatment often spares them from unnecessary anxiety. But also knowledge makes it possible for them to accept the moral responsibility of caring for themselves insofar as they are able. Physicians and nurses can help evoke this sense of responsibility by including the patient as a member of the health care team. As one patient, a heart attack victim, put it, "we were like a team and this was a campaign. I was a member of the team. I was the cause of all the trouble but I was also a member of the team. We were holding hands." As a result of this experience, one would expect greater cooperation between patient, physician, and nurse because they had achieved a "communality" in which the patient/physician and patient/nurse relationship had become "a *covenant* and not a contract" (Zaner, 1985, pp. 88, 101–102). This moral covenant should hold even after the patient has left the hospital and assumed the moral responsibility for his own care with the guidance and advice of his physician and nurse. Doubtless, this relationship would be improved if patients could choose their own nurse, but the covenant is in the nature of the relationship, not the setting in which the relationship occurs.

Patients expect their physicians to fulfill the primary moral sense of their profession in that they expect them to really care for them. Zaner (1985) forcefully states this moral imperative.

> Patients want to know that those who care for them really care. To be sick or injured is to experience ourselves as diminished, as afflicted to various degrees and in precisely those ways which mark us as distinctively human: in our freedom to choose and act, our ability to think and imagine and plan, the intimacy of our relatedness to our own bodies and minds, and our relatedness to other persons. To want to know and to be really cared for, as afflicted, is a uniquely demanding moral phenomenon (p. 98).

Patients do expect nurses and physicians to act from the moral sense in care for the ill, but do patients have an obligation to care for others who are ill? For example, one patient suffering from multiple fractures as a result of an automobile accident had an extremely serious injury to her back. During her rehabilitation and therapy, she made rounds in the wheelchair to comfort other patients and organize group singing for them. Certainly, when a patient who is suffering from illness or accident comforts and entertains other ill persons, this is acting from the moral sense in its highest form.

The above example of care for the ill would not be regarded as exceptional for a well person, however. We expect well persons to visit and comfort the ill. The moral sense of benevolence is evident in this cultural expectation. But we make exceptions for the ill and injured. We expect them to be self-centered in their preoccupation with their pain, suf-

fering, treatment, and prognosis. If a patient stoically en-
dures pain, cooperates with physicians and nurses, and assumes responsibility for fostering his or her own healing,
we normally consider that patient to have fulfilled the expectations for a morally good patient. Thus our moral expectations of an ill person are different from those of a well
person.

When patients who cannot recover completely are
faced with living with chronic illness or debilitation, our
moral expectation of them also changes. But what of their
moral expectations of themselves? Certainly, a person who
was formerly the family bread winner, but can no longer be,
faces a moral crisis concerning the worth of his or her life.
Then the moral sense operates in a very different context.
How the moral sense can operate in even very restricted
contexts was evident in the case of the woman dying with
cancer who gave comfort and assurance to the young nursing student who was caring for her. Do debilitation and
chronic illness suspend the moral sense or merely alter its
direction? This issue is raised in the American movie,
"Whose Life Is It Anyway?" A quadraplegic who could no
longer be a sculptor decided he had the right to discontinue
the technical support that kept him living. But Richard
Dreyfus' portrayal of the lead character, especially of his relationship to other persons, implied that he had much to
give because of his intelligence and ability to communicate
with others. In contrast, the same character in the British
version seemed to have only the choice between death and
continuing a meaningless life. Thus, the British version of
the film raised the question of the right to take one's life. In
contrast, the American version poses the question, "Does
one have the right to take his life when he obviously has
much to give to others, even in his limited condition?" Put
differently, is the moral sense suspended when one can no
longer pursue the chosen direction of his life and must work
in very restrictive conditions? Or does the moral sense require that the disabled and chronically ill ask, "What can I
give to others in the limited condition of my life now?"

When patients do recover from illness, Zaner believes

that they have a moral obligation to those who are ill. He quotes Albert Schweitzer who contends that illness "seems uniquely capable . . . of awakening 'a moral sense that is usually dormant but that on special occasions can be brought to the surface'" (Zaner, 1985, p. 102). In commenting on the reflections of a forty-two-year-old coronary bypass patient who had recovered a new zest for life during his illness and treatment, Zaner (1985) observed that

> there is something else here which also is remarkable: gratitude. He is, of course, (as is plain in his earlier remarks), grateful to his wife and family for "putting up" with him and sticking by him, to the physicians and surgeons and nurses (for the most part), and to the technologies that made it possible for him to recover. But he is also grateful for his "total experience," for having recovered "new values" and a new sense of priorities—of what is truly important for him (p. 103).

This sense of gratitude coming after the experience of pain, uncertainty, and frustration unites former patients together as Schweitzer clearly saw.

> All through the world, there is a special league of those who have known anxiety and physical suffering. A mysterious bond connects those marked by pain. They know the terrible things man can undergo; they know the longing to be free of pain. Those who have been liberated from pain must not think they are now completely free again and can calmly return to life as it was before (Zaner, 1985, p. 103).

Having recovered from anxiety, physical suffering and pain, former patients, according to Zaner, have an obligation to those who will undergo the misfortunes they have recently endured.

> Being marked by the gratefulness of recovery seems to bear a moral meaning that is often undetected and unencouraged. Our good fortune in being enabled by others to recover obligates: this good luck which befalls the patient,

no less than the illness itself, must not (as Schweitzer says) be taken for granted, its burden muted or forgotten. For now, having been ill and having recovered, patients are obligated to give something in return to others, especially to those who now find themselves marked by pain, anxiety, and suffering and long to be free of them (p. 104).

That patients are responding to this moral obligation is evident in the number of help groups, such as Alcoholics Anonymous, Reach to Recovery, Colostomy Clubs, and others.

In summary some patients have a moral sense of being patients and of gratitude for the health care they receive. The primary expression of this moral sense by patients is appreciation and acknowledgment of good care. However, the moral sense also is implicit in the patient's trusting and patient attitude toward the physician and nurse. Although the moral sense of patients has been inadequately developed as a cultural expectation, the moral sense has important implications for the way in which patients relate to each other while ill, for persons who return to the everyday world with chronic illness or debilitation, and for the relationship of persons who have recovered from illness to persons who become ill.

The moral sense expressed by patients is remarkable, especially in light of the absence of a cultural expectation fostering this sense, lack of concrete direction for expressing it, and minimal encouragement by nurses, physicians, and others to evoke the moral response to being a patient. One aspect of the moral sense of nursing which has been neglected is showing appreciation when patients express the moral sense in the way they face suffering and cooperate with nurses in caring for themselves. Another aspect is failing to relate to patients in a way that evokes a moral response to their illness so as to help restore their full humanity, which is threatened by illness and debilitation.

Of course, fostering and articulating the moral sense in patients could be regarded as another moral duty imposed on over-worked nurses by ethicists from outside nursing. But to take this position would be to miss the point of this chapter. The moral sense is already implicit in nursing practice itself. Indeed, what is remarkable about nursing as it is now practiced is the strong moral sense immanent within it. The moral imperative which undergirds nursing practice is threatened from outside by those who would transform nursing into an applied science concerned primarily with technique. Unfortunately, many who are concerned about morality and nursing are turning to ethicists for the techniques required to make moral decisions in nursing practice. Ironically, this tendency can lead the nurse to focus on the technical aspects of ethics and miss the moral sense already inherent in nursing. Learning to apply ethics is often experienced as an added burden to over-worked nurses. However, when the moral sense inherent in practice is articulated as an ethic of practice, it is not experienced as an added duty because realizing the moral sense in concrete nurse-patient relationships is what makes nursing fulfilling.

Chapter 7

The Moral Sense and Nursing Ethics

Nursing ethics would seem to be simply a practical matter if the moral sense is intrinsic to and foundational for nursing practice. Then, nurses would fulfill their moral obligations by excellent practice which would, of course, foster the physical and psychological well-being of patients. Excellent practice is, indeed, the primary moral imperative for nurses. But, if excellent practice is the primary moral imperative for nurses, why is there so much emphasis on nursing ethics and why are nursing schools employing ethicists? The answer usually given is that nurses need the assistance of experts in ethics to help them resolve moral problems in nursing practice by using the moral norms and means of appraisal developed by philosophers to make judgments concerning these problems. If this approach is in the bioethical tradition, then the problems are apt to be attributed to advances in medical science and technology. Thus, both the "cause" of the problem and the means of resolving it are imported into nursing practice from outside of practice. In contrast, if the moral sense is inherent in nursing, then moral problems appear in everyday practice and are resolvable from within practice. This is not to say that some moral problems are not magnified by advances in medical technology and science or that nurses might not benefit from con-

---

This chapter includes material excerpted from *Advances in Nursing Science*, Vol. 9, No. 3, pp. 34–43, with permission of Aspen Publishers, Inc., © April 1987.

sidering the moral norms and ways of making judgments of philosophers or other ethicists. But since moral problems are inherent in nursing practice itself, their articulation and resolution should occur in terms of practice.

When the moral sense of nursing is taken seriously, then nursing ethics becomes clinical ethics. In clinical ethics, as Richard Zaner (1988) points out, moral issues are situationally defined and treated contextually within health care practice. In addition, the primary resources for resolving moral issues are not outside experts but the participants themselves, i.e., nurses, physicians, patients and others with a legitimate interest.

If nursing has a moral sense which requires clinical ethics, does this not mean that nursing ethics boils down to excellent practice? If this is so, why are there moral problems which are not merely a matter of the quality of practice? First, nurses do not always follow the moral sense inherent in nursing practice. For example, sometimes nurses place their own professional advancement or comfort above the well-being of the patient. This, however, is not peculiar to nurses. All human beings face the problem of actually doing what they ought to do for others rather than advancing their self-interest. But when nurses do this, they are different from those whose practices do not have a dominant moral sense, for example, salesmen, because when nurses act out of self-interest, they reject the major intentionality of their practice. This problem is not a "how to" problem which can be resolved with the proper moral norms and procedures for making ethical judgments. Paul Sharkey (1986) addresses this issue directly by asking the age old question, "Can morality be taught?" (p. 7) His answer is that it cannot be taught but it can be caught. Novices will not learn to be moral by being taught how to make moral judgments by ethicists. According to Sharkey, commitment to the moral sense of medical practice can be evoked by working in clinical situations with teacher-physicians who exemplify the moral sense in their practice (p. 7).

Sharkey's insight has important implications for nursing education. Certainly, if the moral sense is as strong as our study indicates that it is, finding teacher-nurses who work from the moral sense should not be difficult. Therefore, the problem is not finding nurse clinicians who work from a moral sense, but rather helping clinicians make apparent to their students the moral sense inherent in nursing practice. Unfortunately, this moral sense is often hidden or obscured. This is, indeed, strange in light of the moral sense which became apparent in Benner's thorough study of nursing competencies and in our study of fulfillment in nursing. Perhaps the reason for this is that, although nurses practice with an implicit moral sense in the background, they articulate their practice almost exclusively in professional and technical language. This implies that the problem in the moral education of nurses is not the lack of clinical teachers who have the moral sense but, rather, that nursing is not articulated in the language of the moral sense. Nurses do, in fact, need to study ethics but not as a philosophical discipline to be *applied* to nursing practice. Instead, nurses need to study clinical ethics so that they can articulate the moral sense inherent in a practice. When this articulation is missing from nursing ethics, nurses often focus on philosophical discussions *about* ethical problems in nursing rather than on fulfilling the moral sense inherent in their own practice.

A second moral issue concerns the reform of nursing practice. After all, some nursing practice always falls short of the moral imperative to promote the well-being of the patient. For example, many veteran nurses remember when direct patient care was ordered by the physician rather than coming under the legitimate authority of the nurse. Nurses have, over the years, actually reformed this practice so that they now make their own decisions concerning better patient care. One on-going reform, which is expanding the legitimate authority of nurses to promote the well-being of patients, is patient education and discharge planning. This reform is being expanded to include an emphasis on the promotion and maintenance of health. Thus, improving practice is a moral imperative for nurses.

Problems related to fulfilling the moral sense of practice and reforming practice are not peculiar to health care or nursing practice. But there are moral dilemmas which are inherent in the nature of medical and nursing practice. These dilemmas concern tensions between (1) what is medically prescribed and the patient's interpretation of the good; (2) the different intentionalities in the various health care professions; (3) objective treatment and personal care; (4) unified care and specialization; and (5) developing personal helping relationships with patients in an institutional and professional context. The first of these dilemmas concerns the tensions between what Pellegrino (1985) calls the medically right decision as determined by the physician and the morally good decision as decided by the patient. Traditionally, many physicians have held that only the medically right treatment should be considered. As a consequence of recent recognition of patients' rights, the patient has a greater role in determining the nature of treatment. Even when the patient's right is clearly acknowledged, however, the patient is still very dependent on the physician's expert knowledge in making a sound choice. Just as the patient is dependent on the physician, the physician is in turn dependent on the patient for his understanding of the patient's wishes. When neither physician nor patient understand each other's position, the moral issue is apt to become one of rights—who has the moral (and legal) right to choose. However, a conflict over rights often obscures the fact that both physician and patient are moral agents. The physician and nurse, no less than the patient, have to concern themselves with what is morally right. As Pellegrino (1985) contends, this requires a dialogical relationship between physician and patient in which they decide together on the treatment which best fulfills the moral sense of benevolent concern for each other (pp. 20–23).

Sara Fry (1986) gives an excellent example of this dilemma in nursing care. In this case, when the patient's stomach cancer did not respond to chemotherapy, the patient and her husband unilaterally decided not only to discontinue chemotherapy but also all intravenous means of providing nutrition and fluids. She wanted to go home with her husband, live as normally as possible, and put her house in order. Although the nurse did not deny the patient's right legally or morally to make that choice, she wrestled with the problem of what to do when the patient's decision would eventuate in death by starvation. She decided that she must inform the patient of what such a death would be like. Also, she concluded that she must help the patient decide what should be done for and to her if she returned to the hospital in a condition in which she could not make her own decisions. Thus, the nurse was able to be morally responsible to the patient when she was torn between what she believed to be the right medical decision and what the patient believed was the good moral decision for her and her husband.

A second moral dilemma results from the conglomerate of intentionalities which have developed over time in the health care professions. Although the dominant sense of health care practice is the moral sense (fostering the well-being of patients), it includes other senses. For example, the economic sense of health care comes from the free enterprise system, namely the "bottom line." The logic of the bottom line—to make as much profit as possible—clearly conflicts with the moral sense of the medical profession. Further, the medical and nursing professions have as one of their aims promoting the well-being of the members of the profession. For example, this intention did indeed work against the moral sense of benevolence when the AMA limited the number and size of medical schools at a time when there was a great shortage of physicians in small towns, rural areas and inner cities and many qualified applicants were denied admission to medical schools. And, one might add, this is a violation of the intention of the free enterprise system in that it restricts trade, thus keeping prices high. However, professions must promote the good of the profession in order to fulfill their mission. For example, one thinks of how the low salaries and prestige of nurses have negatively affected the quality of nursing care. Tymieniecka (1984) suggests how the conglomeration of intentionalities in the health professions can be dealt with while keeping the focus on the moral sense of benevolence. This can be accomplished through the *"value preference mode* in which we attribute to each of the conflicting elements its *due"* (p. 32).

Giving "each of the conflicting elements its due" is often very difficult in health care because the moral sense embedded in practice must work through a network of social and legal rights and privileges which regulate the relationships of physician, nurse, and patient. For example, physicians have legal rights to diagnose and prescribe treatment to patients. What happens when these rights conflict with the moral obligations of the nurse is evident in the case of *Tuma v. Board of Nursing of State of Idaho* (1979). Tuma was an instructor in a college nursing program. She and a nursing student were caring for a patient who had a diagnosis of leukemia and had an order for chemotherapy. The patient confided to Tuma that she had had success in treating her disease for twelve years through the practice of religion. Tuma subsequently discussed with the patient alternative treatments to chemotherapy, including natural products. In the end, the patient continued with her chemotherapy and later died. The physician, believing Tuma's conduct to be improper, reported her to the State Board of Nursing, which charged her with unprofessional conduct—a charge which was upheld in the initial trial. Although the decision was overturned by the Court of Appeals, it was on a technicality, thus not altering the court's support of the physician's authority. The Tuma case made clear the legal right of the physician to prescribe treatment. But what of the patient's right to seek medical advice elsewhere? And what of the nurse's right to give counsel, when requested, which does not prescribe treatment but suggests other possible treatments?

To focus this issue more clearly, consider the following imaginative variation. A patient does not want to follow the *only* treatment her physician will prescribe for her incurable cancer. At best, following that, or any, treatment, she can live from a few months to a year. The treatment her physician prescribes would be very costly and would involve spending most of her remaining life in a hospital. Morally she does not want to burden her family financially, and personally, she wants to spend as much time as possible at home with her family. She asks her nurse, who knows well her wishes, if there are other types of treatment available. From her experience, the nurse knows that other competent physicians have, in fact, prescribed other treatments and shares this information with the patient. The patient consults with another physician and chooses a treatment which is more in accord with her moral sense and personal desires. Clearly, this is a case in which the physician's legal right to prescribe the professionally "right" treatment is in conflict with the good of the patient and the moral sense of the nurse.

The third dilemma in health care practice concerns the tension between the objective intentionality of science and technology and interpersonal care based on benevolence. Gadow (1985) put this issue very clearly.

> The reason, then, that technology poses a greater threat to dignity than does less complex care is related to the experience of otherness. Mundane care and simple apparatus involve measures that persons usually can manage for themselves. But complicated measures and machinery are more disruptive; they can remove the locus of control and of meaning from the individual by imposing otherness in two forms, the machine and the professional: (1) the apparatus asserts an otherness that cannot be ignored or easily integrated into the physical or psychological being of the person, and (2) complex techniques require greater expertise than many persons possess, and professionals may be called in to manage the procedure (p. 35).

Gadow contends that this objectification of the patient does not simply result from the use of technology but from the consciousness that informs professional medicine. The patient is regarded as an instance of a disease categorically defined and as a problem to be solved. For example, Chris Sizemore, whose case was treated in the movie, "The Three Faces of Eve," reports that although her mental illness was important enough to "make a motion picture about," she felt that she was "so unimportant I didn't even tell people who I was" (*Daily Advance*, p. 27). Gadow (1985) contends that the resolution of this problem requires understanding care in a new way. For her "caring is attending to the 'object-ness' of persons without reducing them to the moral status of objects" (pp. 33–34). She contends that treating patients as subjects rather than objects requires touching them as fel-low human beings and speaking with them concerning the meaning and implication of their treatment and illness. Gadow also contends that objectivity enters health care as professional methodology. Health care professionals have developed routine procedures for handling certain cases and accomplishing certain tasks. Thus, health care comes to have two meanings. The first is routine professional care learned in professional schools of medicine and nursing. The second is personal care for this particular person who is ill. In the Tuma case these two senses of care came into conflict—the physician demanding that routine profes-sional procedures be followed and Tuma responding from the spontaneous moral sense to the specific request of a par-ticular ill person.

The fourth moral dilemma concerns the giving of uni-fied care to patients by professionals who are fractured by the various specialities within medicine and nursing. Some professionals have sought this unity through the use of theories. For example, Neuman (1982) contends that sys-tems theory can restore unity to nursing practice. Some seek unity in holistic medicine which calls for physicians, nurses, social workers, psychologists, and clergymen to work together in one comprehensive program of health care. But holistic attempts at unity often fail because, as Ty-mieniecka (1984) has pointed out, they don't take seriously the divisions and conflicts within practice itself. She con-tends that true unity comes from recapturing the moral sense implicit in practice. Certainly, health care should be holistic concerning medical treatment and direct care in that nurses, physicians, patients, and others with legitimate interests and authority need to work together in making decisions concerning medical treatment and direct care. But the primary way to achieve this unity is not to adopt a holistic approach but to cultivate a common devotion to the well-being of the patient which takes precedence over allegiance to a special field of expertise or devotion to a particular health care profession. Thus, a moral imperative for nurses is contributing their particular expertise and talents to common programs of health care which foster the well-being of patients.

The fifth dilemma concerns tensions in developing and maintaining personal helping relationships with patients in an institutional and professional context. Zaner (1988, pp. 251–264) describes three such dilemmas in physician-patient relations, which nurses also face. The first is the dilemma of health care professionals and patients meeting as strangers and yet being interdependent. Often physicians know their patients professionally, whereas nurses in many settings are assigned to patients whom they do not know. Yet nurses usually relate to patients much more closely than physicians. Most nurses understand one side of this dilemma in that they know that patients are dependent on them and that patients need to trust and cooperate with them. However, they often fail to realize that good patient care requires that nurses trust and cooperate with patients. The moral sense requires both patient and nurse to learn to trust and cooperate with each other even though they initially meet as strangers in a professional relationship.

The second dilemma occurs because nurses must establish personal relationships with the patient which involve caring for and helping the patient, but at the same time, must maintain efficient work schedules. Clinical ethics requires the nurse to learn how to balance personal relationships with work efficiency.

The third dilemma results from the necessity of a nurse to be able to relate closely to her patients and at the same time to distance herself from patients. For example, while a nurse must be able to relate personally to the patient, she must at the same time distance herself enough from her patients so that their suffering and dying will not inhibit her professional care or destroy her as a person. This indicates why they must learn to walk what Sally Tisdale (1986) has vividly described as a "narrow trail flanked by extremity." On one side is empathetic relationship, "filled with wrenching sorrow, anger and despair," and "on the other side is a kind of total severance from the person in pain" which is "more than detachment" (p. 129).

Distancing is also required because of the tension between personal disclosure and the situation of the nurse. In everyday personal relationships when one partner discloses something about her personal life, the other partner usually responds in kind. Nurses require intimate disclosure from their patients but usually do not and often should not make such disclosures about themselves to their patients. The moral sense requires the nurse to remember that "one is always a stanger and a guest when another's subjective experience is concerned" (Zaner, 1988, p.261) and to relate to her patients accordingly.

Dilemmas by their nature cannot be solved; they simply must be faced. However, they need not be faced alone. Tisdale movingly describes the need for help in facing dilemma in a burn unit.

> Along the narrow road, where the nurses scrape little Michael's naked nerves, is a simple acceptance. Here is now, this is happening, keep walking. To project another's experience onto oneself (how would *I* feel; what if this were my child?) is both terribly necessary and terribly dangerous. Burn nurses work here year after year, anonymously, cutting off skin and treading lightly. It is easy to slip. They must help each other up when they fall (Tisdale, 1986, pp. 129–130).

To give this needed support, Zaner suggests that health care workers need to establish networks of support and criticism. This would mean that nurses should not only be willing to support and criticize each other but should establish communities of nurses and perhaps other health care workers who will assist them in facing dilemmas. Criticism within communal support is necessary to prevent mistakes with which nurses would find it difficult to live. When such mistakes occur, nurses need the support of their fellow nurses in order to profit from their mistakes and at the same time to recover their sense of well-being. Such support is often not given. In an example given by Zaner, a pediatrician who makes an understandable mistake in an operation which leads to a child's death, receives support, not from his fellow physicians, but from the child's parents. The parents said that the medical and nursing staffs were "good folks who wouldn't deliberately harm anyone" (Zaner, 1988, p. 259). Nurses should also be "good folks" in that they are willing to criticize and support their fellow nurses within a sense of community.

Zaner (1988) also suggests that one way of coping with these dilemmas is learning to communicate better with patients. This requires translating professional and technical language into the everyday language and situation of the patient. It also requires listening to the patient and creating an atmosphere and situation in which the patient feels free to speak his mind. Zaner gives an excellent example of failure to create such an atmosphere in the following excerpt from a tape recording of a patient's remarks.

> I know . . . [clears throat] . . . I know now that no matter . . . how long my sentence is . . . it's gonna be spent in a nursing home, alone . . . 's far as my family is concerned. But I'm glad they don't have to sit and watch me die. I had to sit and watch Mother die, an' it was terrible. I think I'll spare my children that . . . not that I have any choice about it. Can't think of a worse way to spend it th' . . . than in a nursing home. Which is just like bein' in jail, really. You have no rights; you're just a number. A baby. An' all the bodies are old and worn out, an' yours is no different than anybody else's. An' I found out that it's not any advantage at all . . . to have your . . . brains left, because, when you question things, they think you're trying to tell them how to run their business. It's better not to question, it's better just t' go 'n accept their discipline like a child would: no questions, just do [long pause while she tries to turn off the machine, then finally succeeds] (Zaner, 1988, p. 268).

Thus, the atmosphere in this patient's nursing home is such that she finds it to be a disadvantage to have "brains left" and feels that she must hide her intelligence in order not to upset the expected routine. From the same tape, Zaner gives another example of how this patient is not really heard.

> Well, here's *another* day . . . I'll swear, how slowly they pass . . . and you wonder why I can't be cheerful about things. I'm trying, I really am tryin', but I'm not gettin' anywhere . . . . When he [her pulmonary specialist] told me that there wasn't any possible chance for me to get out and have another apartment on my own . . . and . . . that I'd always have to live in a place like this . . . that . . . that did somethin' to me . . . I really couldn't shake it. I know I'm gloomy and sad, an' all that. You'll just have to bear with me . . . I may get used to it, an' I may not . . . 'ts a bad deal. . . . (Zaner, 1988, p. 268).

In spite of the fact that this patient has been put into a nursing home and is actually dying, she is expected to be "happy, happy" by those she encounters. But are the only alternatives false optimism or severe depression? Zaner points out that this patient needs to learn to face her situation and discover the possibilities for a meaningful life that remain to her. Nurses usually, more than any other caretakers, are in a better position to help patients understand their "*situated meaning*" (Benner and Wrubel, 1989, p. 15) and to discover and fulfill their "situated possibilities" (p. 16).

One way in which the moral sense differs from traditional nursing ethics is that it directs us to moral dilemmas which cannot be solved but must be lived with and, when possible, ameliorated. Ethicists in the applied bioethics tradition often focus on problems to be solved rather than on practice and, thus, tend to miss these dilemmas. These dilemmas can be avoided by neglecting one's moral responsibility. For example, a nurse might resolve the distancing dilemma by becoming so distant from her patients that she would not relate to them personally or with compassion. On the other hand, a nurse might become so personally involved with patients that she does not work efficiently or professionally. In practice, a nurse knows that she is morally responsible when she feels the tension between being responsive to particular patients and being efficient or between personally relating to patients and maintaining a professional distance. After all, the first moral requirement of a nurse is excellent practice, and excellent practice requires all four senses of caring which Pellegrino advocates. A nurse must be compassionate, give direct care, be professionally competent, and use the craftsmanship of nursing with efficiency and diligence. But it is difficult to be compassionate and give direct care and, at the same time, to use the knowledge, skill, and craftsmanship of nursing demanded by professional care. This is especially so in a time in which advances in medical science and technology are placing so many new professional demands on nurses which cause tension in maintaining their tradition of compassion and direct care.

As we have seen, Zaner, by working from within practice itself, discloses moral dilemmas in practice which traditional medical ethicists often miss in their zeal to *solve* moral problems. But he also shows that the stress on rights and autonomy, so pervasive in contemporary medical ethics, is philosophically unsound. Zaner questions philosophically whether any ethic can be based primarily on the conviction that "each individual person is a free and autonomous agent" (Zaner, 1988, p. 286). For Zaner there are two questionable assumptions which underlie the idea of the autonomous self.

1. The self is essentially closed on itself. It is insulated and capable of thinking only its own thoughts and feeling only its own feelings.
2. The only direct experience one self has of another person is sensory experience of the other's body. Hence, the other person is not experienced in any direct way, but must rather be somehow inferred on the basis of the self's own sensory experiences (since all that is directly experienced is the other's *body*) (Zaner, 1988, p. 288).

Nurses know that the above assumptions are unsound from their own experience. If the self is autonomous, in that it is closed in on itself, and therefore unable to grasp another person's meaning directly, nursing as practiced would be impossible. If a nurse can only infer meaning from a person's bodily movement rather than grasp the meaning from the body's expressiveness, nursing practice would certainly have to be altered. Imagine trying to turn a patient on a bed with efficiency and care to avoid unnecessary suffering if each grimace, body tension, grunt and moan, was to be taken as a sign from which to infer what was going on inside the body and then be correlated to the appropriate technique inferred from each sign. Instead, most nurses immediately recognize what the patient's bodily expressions mean and move him appropriately drawing on long years of practical experience. Of course, some might object to the claim that nurses can read a patient's bodily movement directly by pointing out that stoic patients often hide their pain and suffering while those with the opposite attitude "feel" pain before they are even touched or moved. But the fact that nurses recognize this indicates that they can indeed read the meanings of bodily expression. Further, they would be unable to identify this behavior as exceptional if the movement of most persons' bodies were not clearly and immediately understood. If we were completely autonomous, we would never be able to know or understand other persons. But the fact that we do understand other persons has important implications for the moral life, as Zaner points out.

> Positively, if we are neither solipsistic in and for ourselves, nor alien and essentially remote from the lives of other persons, but are instead with others at every point (though in many different ways), then it is not insularity and autonomy that define our being but rather togetherness and mutuality.
>
> Moral life is not first of all a matter of the isolated "rational will" functioning in and of itself to provide itself with self-authorized and self-sufficient governance (autonomy = auto + nomos), and then, on that basis relating to other persons in ways dictated by the self-derived moral law. To the contrary, moral life is essentially com-

munal at its root, and it is mutuality (in all its complex forms), not autonomy, that is foundational. Nowhere is this more plainly evident than in the contexts of clinical situations dealing with ill persons (Zaner, 1988, p. 292).

Zaner is certainly right in contending that clinical situations make evident both the inadequacy of the autonomous approach to ethics and the strength of the mutuality approach. Quite apart from Zaner, our own search for an ethic appropriate to the moral issues nurses face in clinical situations led us to the conclusion that stress on rights and autonomy tends to obscure and inhibit the cooperative moral decision-making required in health care practice, whereas stress on togetherness and mutuality fosters and enhances making those decisions. We will show why the autonomy approach is inadequate by critically appraising the contention of Roland Yarling and Beverley McElmurry (1986) that the crucial issue in nursing ethics is autonomy. Then, we will show that the in-between situation of nurses, which is so abhorent to those who stress autonomy, is, in fact, a privileged position for affecting the cooperative moral decisions required by sound health care practice. We will contrast our ethic of practice, i.e., an ethic developed within health care practice, with Yarling's and McElmurry's (1986) applied ethic. Rather than beginning with the lived moral sense of nursing, Yarling and McElmurry begin with academic moral decision-making as it is taught in typical ethics courses. Ethicists have traditionally argued that one acts morally by bringing one's actions under the control of a moral norm which defines the good, such as psychic harmony (Plato), self-realization (Aristotle), acting on duty (Immanuel Kant), and giving pleasure and preventing pain (John Stuart Mill). To act in accordance with a moral norm, one needs autonomy. Therefore, autonomy becomes a necessary condition for acting morally. Yarling and McElmurry (1986) contend that nurses lack sufficient autonomy to be moral agents. To support their position, they usually choose examples in which the nurse acts on behalf of the patient in tension or conflict with physicians and/or hospital bureaucrats (p. 68–70). Since in these examples nurses obviously lack autonomy, Yarling and McElmurry contend that nurses can only truly be moral agents when the health care system has been reformed so that nurses can act as autonomous individual professionals. In fact, they contend that nurses need to be less concerned with traditional personal ethics and more focused on reform of the system.

Yarling and McElmurry, like many in modern medical ethics, especially bioethics, stress structural and conceptual moral issues to the neglect of the moral issues in everyday practice. This is unfortunate, especially when examining professions that have a foundational moral sense, such as nursing. Since nursing practice aims at the well-being of the patient, the first moral responsibility of any nurse is excellent practice. Rather than beginning with the everyday moral responsibilities of the nurse to the patient, Yarling and McElmurry focus on situations which require heroic action by the nurse against the establishment. For them, nurses should reform the system so that individual heroic action is not necessary for nurses to be moral agents. But what of the night nurses with too many patients, too few resources, and too little support, who, in spite of the circumstances, give excellent routine care? Are they not to be called moral because they do not have the type of autonomy which Yarling and McElmurry find a necessary condition for morality? Would these nurses not be considered moral, if under such trying conditions, they were pleasant and gave personal support to confused, suffering patients? Obviously, this would constitute excellent practice. In fact, Benner (1984) would call the above the work-role competency of: "Coping with staff shortages and high turnover: Maintaining a caring attitude toward patients even in the absence of close and frequent contact" (p. 147). Although Benner is describing the competencies of nursing excellence, this competency is a description of how nurses fulfill the moral sense of nursing. Such moral action is now being taken by nurses without additional autonomy or reform of the health care system. According to Yarling and McElmurry, reform of the health care system is more morally significant than individual care for patients. Of course, nurses should seek reform which would change such conditions as those described above, but labelling excellent care as *merely* personal moral action misses the moral sense inherent in nursing practice.

What Yarling and McElmurry call merely personal action is, in fact, as in the above case, nurses working within the system of relationships which constitute the hospital and to which they belong and make their own particular contributions. But for Yarling and McElmurry, the hospital is viewed as an institution rather than as a network and/or community of persons. Indeed, in discussing this lack of autonomy, the authors develop such an "us" and "them" logic that the nurses seem not to be a part of the hospital community.

Their "us" and "them" logic prevents them from giving adequate support to some of their contentions which seem to us to be sound. For example, Yarling and McElmurry claim that there are two necessary conditions for nurses "to be free to be moral" (p. 66). The two necessary conditions are "(1) the emergence of a strong sense of professional autonomy and (2) a shift in the locus of accountability from the physician to the patient" (p. 66). Both of these conditions seem desirable when put within the context of making moral decisions in nursing practice which includes relationships with physicians and other hospital personnel, as well as patients. Indeed, this *should be* the context of nursing practice from which Yarling and McElmurry discuss nursing ethics. When this context is ignored, autonomy is treated abstractly, and its relationship to competence and recognized authority is neglected. When treated contextually, what they call autonomy would be more appropriately designated legitimate authority. Perhaps their abstract treatment of autonomy accounts for their logically odd claim that nurses will gain greater autonomy by being more accountable to their patients. They appear not to be arguing for greater autonomy for the nurse but for a shift in accountability from physician to patient so that the nurse can become the patient's advocate. Such a shift would obviously be an improvement if it increased the nurse's legitimate authority to work with her patients without unwarranted interference from physicians or bureaucrats, but it would not necessarily increase the nurse's autonomy. Obviously, they do not recognize that being accountable to the patient could threaten the nurse's autonomy by patients making unreasonable demands upon the nurse to perform non-professional activities, such as housekeeping, personal favors, and personal relationships inappropriate to nurse-patient relationships. In fact, in the previously cited study which we conducted to determine when nurses felt most and least fulfilled, we found that the nurses felt least fulfilled because of inappropriate demands and abusive treatment by patients far more often than from restrictions by and conflicts with hospital bureaucrats and physicians. In other words, the nurses felt least fulfilled when the demands made by patients conflicted with the legitimate authority of the nurse as a professional. Indeed, one could argue that one of the primary moral obligations of a nurse is to sustain excellent practice in the face of unreasonable demands which deny the legitimate authority of nurses. If nurses were hired by patients directly, as Yarling and McElmurry recommend, then the patient could fire them for not acceding to their demands. Certainly, this is not generally the case now because most nurses work for an institution which protects them from unreasonable patient demands.

Institutions afford security, stable financial support, facilities and resources to the members. If one receives these benefits, then one usually pays a price—often, loss of some individual freedom. As Socrates pointed out long ago, for a person to be free to make autonomous moral criticism and judgment, he must remain a private citizen. In fact, Socrates went so far as to suggest that such a person should not be paid. But it must be remembered that Socrates had many wealthy young students who indirectly contributed to his financial well-being! Our serious point is that if one accepts the protection, salaries, and facilities of an institution, then one sacrifices some individual autonomy. But, the loss of such autonomy does not necessarily require the sacrifice of legitimate authority as a member of a health care team. The question of legitimate authority is certainly begged by statements such as "nursing commitment to patients and autonomy in the exercise of that commitment" is so strong that "few nurses graduating from basic nursing education programs in the past ten years think they owe physicians anything other than professional excellence in practice" (Yarling and McElmurry, 1986, p. 67). Does professional excellence not require following the directions of a physician in certain circumstances? After all, the physician does have the legitimate authority to prescribe medications and treatments, and one function of nurses is to carry out the treatment regimen as prescribed by the physician. Of course, the authors, with their stress on autonomy "in the face of the enemy," discuss only cases in which the nurse recognizes that the physician is giving questionable treatment. They rightly point out that in these cases the nurse is in a precarious position when his moral sense calls for whistle-blowing, especially concerning a physician. However, the tone of their article suggests that nurses are somehow alone in this dilemma. Not only do workers in industries, government and private agencies face the same moral dilemma, physicians also do. Indeed, anyone who knows the "subculture of the health care professions" (Yarling and McElmurry, p. 67) recognizes that physicians cannot whistle-blow on each other without impunity. Our point is certainly not that physicians are in the same precarious position as nurses, but that the moral dilemma of whistle-blowing is inherent in working within any social institution. Yarling and McElmurry show well the individual side of this dilemma, however, they do not discuss the fact that social institutions, in order to be effective, must maintain the trust of the public and harmonious working relationships between the various participants. But more importantly, institutions must protect the legitimate authority of practitioners, not only from other practitioners, but from patients and clients as well. Our sympathies are generally on the side of the "angels" (nurses, patients and rebels), but, unlike Yarling and McElmurry, we must grudgingly admit that the "devils" (physicians, hospital bureaucrats, and defenders of the establishment) have legitimate authority which must be worked with and through if the patient's good is to be promoted.

When Yarling and McElmurry (1986) talk about the autonomy of the profession, they talk as if this means freedom from coercion by the hospital as an institution without saying what the institution is. Do they mean bureaucrats, boards, or physicians? Are nurses not an important and powerful force within the hospital? Have nurses well used what authority they actually or potentially have? Yarling and McElmurry imply that nurses would exercise their autonomy without being self-serving and that the reasons for their present lack of authority is due to physicians, bureaucrats and some nefarious institution called a hospital. They fail to ask whether nurses could not also be as self-serving as physicians and bureaucrats, or whether part of their present dilemma is due to their own lack of asserting both their professional and moral commitments. Is it the case that the "devils" (i.e., the hospital and/or the physicians) are preventing the "saints" (i.e., the nurses) from promoting the good of the patient? John Dewey once called this the "devil theory" of history. He claimed that people looked for some "devil" they could defeat to right the wrongs of the world, rather than to face their own problems and attempt to resolve them.

Physicians and hospital bureaucrats have the same moral commitment as nurses in that they are to promote the physical and psychological well-being of the patient. This means that when they do their job well, by exercising their legitimate authority to promote patient well-being, they are engaging in a moral good. This becomes evident when contrasted with a vocation which has no such moral sense. For example, a used car sales manager, after telling his philosopher-friend that he could not in good conscience sell him any car on his lot, asked his friend to discuss the moral dilemma he faced in selling these cars to unsuspecting customers in order to support his family. Health care professionals do not face this dilemma because their practice has a moral sense. Yarling and McElmurry seem to forget that health care workers, other than nurses, are governed by the same moral norm as they are. They are not like the used car salesman, who as a manager, is governed by the business sense of the "bottom line." Indeed, one worry in the health care profession is that the new for-profit hospitals will be governed by a bottom-line logic rather than the moral sense. This is not to say that some hospital bureaucrats and physicians do not put their professional well-being, material enhancement, and ego-building ahead of the moral imperative of their profession, but then, so do some nurses! But when they do, they violate the moral sense inherent in their practice.

Legitimate Authority vs. Autonomy

Each health care profession has its own legitimate authority which aims at promoting the well-being of the patient. Thus, what Yarling and McElmurry (1986) call moral autonomy might be better thought of as legitimate professional authority. In exploring the nature of health care professions, Pellegrino (1985) reminds us that "professional" means professing (p. 28). The patient comes to the nurse or physician seeking help and the nurse and physician profess to be able to offer that help. For Pellegrino that profession means not only the knowledge and the skill needed to help the patient but commitment to and compassion for the patient as well. This means that most legitimate professional authority grows from within health care professions, rather than from reform of bureaucratic structure and rules which regulate professions. So to talk as if one cannot have legitimate authority without being given autonomy is to misdirect the major moral thrust of nursing.

From within health care practice it makes more sense to talk about legitimate authority than autonomy. For example, physicians have the authority to diagnose disease and to prescribe treatment especially related to drugs and surgery. Nurses do not have the authority to make the same decisions as physicians, but nurses have their own particular kind of authority. Nurses have the authority and power which comes from the control of the day-to-day care of the patient. After all, it was this control that led the patients in "One Flew Over the Cuckoo's Nest" to label the Big Nurse as "big" in comparison to others on the staff of the hospital including the psychiatrists (Kesey, 1973). A positive example of the use of this power to expand legitimate authority occurred when nurses in one hospital over time effected a program instructing patients on how to care for themselves after discharge. Although this program was within the nurse's legal authority some physicians were reluctant to "allow" nurses to teach patients about their diseases and its care after discharge because they doubted the nurse's ability to give correct information. As a result of compromise the nurses were able to do limited teaching at first, but over time they expanded the program until they were teaching what they originally requested. This change was not brought about by a prior sweeping reform which allowed the nurses to assert complete autonomy but by compromise and change which gradually occurred through those who controlled the day-to-day care. In other words, policy is not changed only in the way which Yarling and McElmurry advocate but often by the gradual change of practice which then becomes hospital policy. Certainly nurses should seek reform which would allow them to exercise their legitimate authority, but in the meantime, they have a moral responsibility to change policy by changing practice in desirable ways. Furthermore, the change of practice, as in the above case, usually convinces those in power that nurses have the competence on which such authority is based. Professional autonomy comes from competence duly recognized by others, for as Lawrence Haworth (1986) says, "Competence is the foundation of autonomy" (p. 2).

Of course nurses face moral decisions in which they seem to lack personal autonomy. In our study of fulfillment of nurses, this sometimes occurred when nurses felt that physicians should let patients die. Some nurses in our study did complain that the physician did not allow them to be their patient's advocate. In each case, they believed the patient's situation was hopeless and that patients were being subjected to needless pain and discomfort and were being treated in ways that were an affront to the patient's dignity as a person. The nurses rightly felt sympathy for the patient and moral indignity at taking part in their treatment. Certainly, as members of the treatment team, their views should be heard and taken seriously. But this does not mean that they should or do have the right to make such decisions autonomously. After all, they are part of a team, each of which has its legitimate authority. The patients should have the right to decide concerning their treatment. In our study these nurses did have the right to be the patient's advocate, because the patient actually had asked them to be allowed to die. Although each nurse believed that the patient's situation was hopeless, such determination should be made by the health care team. After all, the patient could be in a temporary situation of extreme pain at the time of the request, but a competent physician might know better than the nurse that this pain would eventually decrease and disappear. Also, the nurse is usually not a better authority than the hospital lawyer on possible litigation that might result if the procedure she is suggesting were carried out. Other questions concerning legitimate authority could be raised, but our point simply is that such decisions have to be team decisions. In these decisions some members of the team have more legitimate authority than others, but no one has complete autonomy. Thus, nurses can best contribute to carrying out the moral sense of health care, not by focusing on autonomy, but by seeking recognition of the legitimate authority of *all* members of the health care team, in ways which promote harmonious, but just, working relationships which promote the well-being of the patient.

Stressing legitimate authority from within health care practice fosters a different approach to nursing ethics than that of Yarling and McElmurry (1986). Although they claim to be developing their nursing ethics from practice, actually their logic seems to come from traditional philosophical normative ethics. In this type of ethical thought, a good action is one which is done in accordance with a moral norm. To act in accordance with a moral norm, one must be free from external restraint, in this case, meaning the hospital or physician. Thus, for nurses to be moral, they must be able to act autonomously. This view of ethics has been attacked by Carol Gilligan (1982) and Nel Noddings (1984) who regard it as a male way of thinking, in contrast to a feminine ethic which is much more situational and relational. Regardless of the significance of gender designation, our contention is that the situational, relational ethic is the one required in health care as practiced.

In previous chapters we have argued that health care ethics begins with the moral sense inherent in health care practice, and that the sense of health care is not given primarily by science, technology or professionalism. Instead, health care begins with illness inhibiting a person's accustomed and desired ways of being in the world. A caring relationship is formed when this person seeks the professional help of the physician or the nurse. In this relationship the physician and nurse promise to use their knowledge and skill for the good of the patient. This requires working together to help the patient achieve his desired way of being, if possible, and if not, to help him make the best of his new situation.

Fostering the well-being of the patient or helping him to adapt to a new situation requires more than medical knowledge and skill. The skill and knowledge must be used in accordance with the moral imperative inherent in health care practice, i.e., for the good of the other. Certainly, neither the physician nor the nurse has the legal or moral right to decide unilaterally what is good for the patient. Although legally the patient has the right to make the decision about what is good for him, morally, that decision should be made by the physician, nurse, and patient working together, because the patient usually needs professional help in deciding what is best for him. This means that health care is not only a moral undertaking in that it aims at the well-being of the patient, but that it also involves communal decision-making by health care workers and the patient who should respect and consider each other's legitimate authority.

As discussed in the previous chapter, nurses recognize the general moral sense of their professional practice as evidenced in our study of the nurses' most fulfilling experiences of nursing. All indicated that they felt most fulfilled when the moral sense of their practice became evident in their direct and/or professional care for patients. It was also evident that their least fulfilling experiences were those in which the well-being of the patient was inhibited by lack of cooperation from patients, physicians, and hospital bureaucrats. Thus, it is understandable that nurses desire more autonomy so that they can make decisions concerning patient care in areas where they have legitimate authority, but many of these decisions must be made in relationship to overall decisions concerning patient care made in cooperation with others on the health care team.

The In-between Situation of Nurses

No doubt the desire to follow the clearcut mandate of promoting the well-being of patients through their day-by-day decisions, free from interference by physicians, bureaucrats and others, fosters the desire for the type of autonomy advocated by Yarling and McElmurry. When Engelhardt pointed out that nurses are, in fact, the persons "in-between" in health care, he meant that they are caught between the traditional authority of the physician, the emerging rights of the patient, and the growing power of hospital bureaucrats. Being caught between these various factions, then, makes it difficult for nurses to make decisions without taking into account the roles, rights, and possible responses of physicians, patients and hospital administration. However, the in-between place of the nurse does not free her from the responsibility of making moral decisions; instead it sets the context in which those decisions must be made.

After all, all those involved in health care are primarily concerned with the well-being of the patient when they follow the moral sense of their vocation. Persons in other vocations may not have the primary sense of their work dictated by the moral sense. The used car salesman, mentioned previously, with strong Christian moral convictions found himself in between a business aimed at making a profit and a Christian conscience which required him to work for the good of others. This is *not* the dilemma of the nurse in making moral decisions with the other professionals with whom she works if all are true to their calling of promoting the well-being of the patient.

In vocations which are not founded on a moral sense, moral issues appear as a consequence of activities aimed at non-moral ends. For example, a company faces such a moral issue when making a product for profit which contains chemicals that endanger the health of workers. In contrast, in such vocations as health care and education, which are moral undertakings by their very nature, the primary moral imperative is excellent practice. For this reason, physicians and nurses sometimes believe that when they carry out their professional activities with competence, efficiency, and professional commitment, they are doing good and need not concern themselves with "other" moral issues. But as we have previously argued, moral issues in health care arise when its moral sense is denied, frustrated, or not adequately fostered for a variety of reasons. One such reason is that health care professions are usually conglomerates containing mixed intentionalities. For example, the moral imperative of medical practice conflicts with its free enterprise fee system, or what is medically correct for the patient differs from the patient's conception of what is morally good, or the good of the profession conflicts with the health care professional's moral obligation to the patient.

In the above cases, moral issues arise as a result of the different intentionalities within single health care vocations, but moral issues also occur because of the different ways in which the moral imperative is built into the various health care professions. Thus, one major source of moral issues in health care concerns conflicting intentionalities related to the perogatives and procedures of the different health care professions. In these conflicts all parties may be guided by the moral sense and face serious moral dilemmas because of the different ways in which they operate. For example, some professionals, like physicians, usually have a clear sense of direction and a clear relationship between their practice and their moral obligation. Nurses, when they exercise their legitimate authority in day-to-day care for patients, as in most of the examples given by Benner, often have self-direction similar to physicians. However, nurses find autonomous self-direction difficult when they work from "in-between" situations.

Engelhardt describes in-between situations as those in which the nurse is *caught*, implying powerlessness and ambiguity. However, being placed in-between the physician, patient and hospital bureaucrat often places the nurse strategically where he can promote good patient care. For example, a physician was in a quandry concerning whether to aspirate the lungs of a patient who was in an advanced stage of metastatic cancer. The patient suffered from hallucinations, and he often experienced severe pain. In addition, due to heavy smoking, the alveoli no longer functioned adequately. The physician believed that the right medical decision was to let the patient die. He did not discuss this with the patient; in fact, he rarely discussed treatment with anyone including nurses. He was a very technically competent surgeon who believed that he alone should determine the medically correct form of treatment. The nurse knew that the patient was weary of his struggle, felt hopeless and was ready to die. But she also knew that for some reason the patient had struggled to remain alive more valiantly than most other patients for whom she had cared. When she complimented him on his remarkable courage, he responded that he was not remarkably courageous at all. He merely wished to remain alive to celebrate Christmas with his family. The patient had a large family with strong attachments to their father and to each other. The family had a tradition of celebrating Christmas together, and Christmas was a few weeks away. In spite of the fact that the nurse knew that this physician did not receive suggestions concerning treatment from nurses "graciously," she shared her knowledge of the patient's wishes with the physician, and he aspirated the lungs. When the patient's loquacious family arrived to

celebrate Christmas, there was much confusion and noise
in the Oncology Unit. Complaints were made by other patients, some of whom were also near the end of their life
and felt they should have peace and quiet during that time
and, of course, their wishes were supported by hospital policy. The nurse, knowing of another patient unit where the
census was very low due to Christmas, arranged for the patient to be transferred to an isolated room on that unit
where other patients would not be disturbed. She even allowed his two-year-old great granddaughter to be "smug-
gled" into the hospital, which at the time was against hospital policy. The dying man fulfilled his final wish because
the nurse worked positively from an in-between situation.

In the above example, the nurse was not "caught" in-between but acted from her privileged in-between position to
foster the good of the patient. Her position made it possible
for her to be an effective patient advocate. This illustrates
why the nurse's in-between stance is a privileged one for
making moral decisions. Since health care is a communal
enterprise, involving patient, physician, nurse, and hospital
administrators, moral decisions in health care require cooperation and accommodation among all involved. The primary actors are patients, physicians, nurses, and hospital
bureaucrats, each of whom has special rights and privileges
secured by law, custom or by the requirements of the situation. Those who contribute to these decisions do so from
different vantage points. When these perspectives function
as they should, they all contribute to the moral sense by fostering the well-being of the patient. However, when the professional sense replaces the moral sense, the well-being of
the patient is no longer the primary goal of the health care.
For example, when the bureaucrat loses the moral sense, the
financial well-being of the institution can be placed above
providing a good setting for health care. Likewise, the physician can place the well-being of the medical profession
above the care of his patient, as can the nurse or the technician. When this happens, the professional sense is placed
above the moral sense. In contrast, morally good decisions
require that the various participants follow the dictates of

the moral sense by contributing their professional understanding and skill to decisions which promote the well-
being of the patient.

In reaching morally good decisions, the nurse works
cooperatively from the vantage point of her expertise, as do
the physician, patient and hospital bureaucrat. However,
the nurse, unlike the others, is in the privileged position
for reaching such decisions because she is accustomed to
deciding from an in-between perspective. The nurse must
faithfully carry out certain orders and prescriptions of the
physician; she is usually closest to the patient in terms of
knowing needs and receiving requests; and she usually
is responsible for maintaining order and hospital policy.
Thus, any moral decision she makes concerning the well-
being of the patient must take all of these factors into consideration. Her "in-between" moral decisions are different
from those of other health care workers, in that she often
decides from an "in-between" situation.

Nurses have two special areas of expertise. Benner well
delineates one area by articulating nursing competencies
from within nursing practice. The other, we have argued, is
the special expertise of knowing how to work in-between
physicians, hospital bureaucrats, and patients. Indeed, this
special in-between talent places a moral imperative on the
nurse to teach dialogical communication and cooperative
decision-making to those in the health care professions
whose pretensions to autonomy have prevented them from
acquiring these talents essential to fulfilling the moral
sense of health care.

Does the unique in-between ambiguous situation of
the nurse cast her in the role of a facilitator of moral decisions, rather than as a maker of them in cooperation with
others? If being a moral agent means making judgments
from moral principles as traditional ethicists have argued,
the nurse *would* be the logical one who fosters compromise.
However, the moral sense is intentional in that it is aimed
at the good of the other through affecting better relationships, situations, and states of affairs in the world. The
moral sense in health care requires promoting physical and

psychological well-being of patients in a given health care context. This context requires that decisions concerning health care be made cooperatively by physician, patient and nurse working in a setting conducive to good health care. To this cooperative decision the physician contributes his professional knowledge and skills, the patient brings his desire for and understanding of a good life, while the hospital administrator provides facilities, equipment and social organization. What does the nurse bring? Does she simply adjudicate between physician, patient and hospital administration? Not if she follows the moral sense which requires cooperative decisions for the good of the patient. Not only does she bring the nursing expertise which Benner has described, her special in-between position places her where she can better contend for needed cooperation, because she shares the medical side of the decision with the physician, the hospital policy side with hospital administration and the personal aspect with the patient. Thus, she is in a more privileged position for making the type of decision that the moral sense of health care requires. In traditional ethics, in which morality means acting on principle or from the right motive, the nurse would, at worst, foster compromise or, at best, facilitate cooperative decisions. But in-between moral decisions are not compromises when understood from the moral sense of the good of the other in concrete situations. The moral sense requires that moral decisions be made in-between. Those who are situated in-between are in a privileged position for fostering such decisions. They are the advocates of communal decisions which bring together expert medical advice and treatment, sound hospital policy and procedure, and the realizable hopes and aspirations of the patient into concrete health care which fosters well-being of the patient.

Doing medical ethics by attempting to reach a consensus for treatment and care by all persons legitimately involved, "may raise difficulties for those sympathetic to more traditional approaches to moral problems," according to Donald Koch (1986, pp. 2–3). He uses William James' treatment of dealing with moral problems to show how such problems come about and can be resolved when there is disagreement between the participants. Actually, James (1948) contends *"that without a claim actually made by some concrete person there can be no obligation, but that there is some obligation wherever there is a claim"* (p. 72). Note how well this fits Pellegrino's moral sense of medical practice. An ill patient seeks the help of a physician; the physician professes to have the understanding and skill the patient needs and to use them to promote his or her well-being. The physician fulfills the moral sense initially by prescribing a medically right treatment. Then, as James and Koch contend, a moral problem would arise when there is a conflicting opinion. For example, the nurse disagrees with the physician concerning the day-to-day care required by the treatment; the treatment requires the hospital administrator to bend hospital policy; the prescribed treatment is not in accord with the patient's view of the good life. When such conflicts arise, the best solution, according to Koch, is for all parties to arrive at a "state of affairs where *everyone makes the same demand" (Koch, 1986, p. 3).* But often the best that can be achieved is "the *de facto* agreement of those persons who take an interest in the question at hand" (p. 3). Koch obviously is describing how moral issues arise and are resolved from within medical practice. But the whole tone of Koch's argument is that often reaching consensus is merely the best we can do. It would be better if we could arrive at "what past philosophers have called 'justified' moral positions" (Koch, 1986, p. 3). But, as it is, according to Koch, often the best that can be done is to muddle along seeking concensus concerning treatment and care. But when viewed from the moral sense of practice, this so-called "muddling through" actually constitutes a justified moral decision, provided that choices are made from *within* the moral sense of sound practice to promote the well-being of the patient.

Obviously, when health care ethics is approached from within health care practice, one makes moral choices very differently than bioethicists or traditional moral philosophers. From within the moral sense of practice, the first moral responsibility of a health care professional becomes excellent practice. Moral issues arise within health care practice when the fulfillment of the moral sense is inhibited. For example, different professional intentionalities often make conflict over legitimate authority more focal than the well-being of the patient. Cooperative use of legitimate authority is necessary in making decisions that foster the well-being of patients. In making these decisions, what often is called compromise should be designated as justified moral decision because it concerns determining sound practice which fosters the well-being of the patient. Thus, nursing ethics, like all health care ethics, rather than being traditional applied ethics, becomes practical ethics or an ethics of practice.

Chapter 8

The Personal Sense of Nursing

The moral and personal sense of nursing are integrally related, as the foregoing treatment of nursing ethics indicates. Nursing practice, after all, primarily concerns the relationship of nurse to patient with contextual relationships involving physicians, hospital administrators and others. As important as these contextual relationships are to nursing practice, the primary relationship is between nurse and patient, as our study of fulfillment in nursing clearly shows. Also, that study indicates that nurses are most fullfilled when the moral sense of nursing is confirmed in a personal relationship with the patient.

The personal sense of nursing concerns a relation between one person who is a nurse and another person who is her patient. Within this relationship, a personal sense of nursing appears when the common practice of nursing is appropriated by the nurse in a way which expresses her personal way of being in relationship to a particular person who is her patient. Thus, the personal relationship of nurse with patient and patient with nurse has a specific structure which is not that of pure personal relations such as friends and lovers.

An excellent description of pure personal relationships, which has significant implications for nursing, has been given by Martin Buber. Buber called this personal relationship *Ich und Du*, which has been translated *I and Thou* by Smith (1958) and *I and You* by Kaufmann (1970). We will use the better known I-Thou with the caution that Thou indi-

145

cates the personal nature of the relationship and not a trans-cendental one. In the I-Thou relationship, according to Buber, the Thou "fills the firmament" in that "everything else lives in *his* light" (Buber, 1923/1970, p. 59). Buber con-trasted this intensely personal relationship with the imper-sonal relationship, I-It. In the I-It relationship, the other is regarded as a thing among things, as Buber puts it, "a dot in the world grid of space and time" (Buber, 1923/1970, p. 59).

Buber's contrast between I-Thou and I-It helps nurses clearly recognize the difference between impersonal, rou-tine professional relationships and personal relationships in nursing practice. For example, those nurses who approach nursing as an application of "scientific" theory and who "care" for their patients as applied scientists, i.e., tech-nologists, fit exactly the relationship which Buber called I-It. In the I-It relationship a person is reduced to a thing through categorization, for example, "the lung cancer in 602." Such relationships are always partial; that is, the nurse limits her relationship to the patient to matters con-cerning the disease. Further, the relationship is established for utilitarian reasons, i.e., so the disease can be cured or treated palliatively. The patient is regarded as a good patient if he does what the nurse wants.

In contrast, when the implication of an I-Thou relation-ship are adapted to nursing practice, the nurse would ask the patient to share mutually in planning for his care. She would regard him as of worth in his own right, regardless of how he responded to her. She would be *present* to him as a whole person who was ill and treat him primarily as a per-son, not as a disease to be cured. Her knowledge would be knowledge of him, growing out of their personal relation-ship. In summary, I-It relationships are one-sided, partial, utilitarian, objectifying and detached. In contrast, I-Thou re-lationships are mutual relationships in which the partners are present to each other as whole persons, each legitimate in his own right.

In the foregoing description of an I-Thou relationship in nursing practice, Buber's description of pure I-Thou relationships has been adapted to fit nursing practice. Without such adaptation, Buber's I-Thou would be inappropriate for nursing practice as we shall show later. But for now, we want to note that nurses often initially respond to Buber's pure I-Thou relationships as impractical. The routine of their work, the demands on their time, and requirements to maintain professional distance from their patients would prevent them from having pure I-Thou relationships with their patients. Buber, himself, recognized the impossibility of being in I-Thou relationships all or most of the time. However, he believed that it was possible to remain in I-It relationships all the time. Therefore, he contended "without *It* man cannot live. But he who lives with *It* alone is not a man" (Buber, 1923/1970, p. 34). Nurses can learn from Buber how personal relationships are demanded by our humanity, how personal relationships contrast with I-It relationships, and how I-It relationships required by our technically oriented society pose threats to I-Thou relationships.

As valuable as Buber's description of I-Thou and I-It is for nurses, most of nursing care cannot be incorporated within Buber's dichotomy between I-Thou and I-It for two reasons. First, although Buber does show the necessity of I-It relationships between persons, he does not indicate what kind of impersonal relationship is appropriate when one person is relating to a person rather than a thing. We will show that this relationship can be appropriately described as an I-It (Thou) relationship. Second, Buber described personal relationships as unstructured relationships which have no end beyond themselves. Nursing is a structured relationship which is established for a definite purpose. Thus, Buber's pure I-Thou relationship is inappropriate, not merely for such mundane reasons as maintaining a routine, etc. but, because of the nature of nursing practice itself. We will show how the purposive relationship between nurse and patient can be structured by practice and yet be personal in Buber's sense of mutual relationships, in which the partners are present to each other as whole persons, each legitimate in his or her own right.

I-It (Thou) Relationships

Buber's description of an I-It relationship clearly shows why impersonal relationships are inappropriate between nurse and patient. Buber's I-It relationship well describes nurses who use a rigid routine often designated as "good professional practice," applicable by *any* nurse to *any* patient regardless of his personal ways, the nature of his illness, or his situation. Thus, the patient becomes merely a body-object—a thing to be treated routinely. But most nurses do not "operate by the book." Even when attending routinely to the body-object, they do not reduce the patient to the moral status of an object. Such relationships between nurse and patient could neither be described as I-Thou or as I-It but could be described as I-It (Thou) (Scudder and Mickunas, 1985).

An I-It (Thou) relationship is one in which a person is recognized as a person, even when limited time, the need for routine precision, or the patient care situation requires impersonal treatment. For example, taking and charting vital signs is done routinely because it saves time, promotes efficiency and communicates directly and clearly to other health care professionals. The fact that this procedure is impersonal does not mean that the nurse should regard the patient primarily as a thing to be treated. The bracketed Thou means that even when dealing with the patient objectively in a very routine manner, the nurse should always be aware that she is relating to a person.

Being aware that a patient is a person is the basis for recognizing patient's rights. Rights, after all, are impersonal. One has rights as a citizen of the state or the nation, as a professional or, in the case of human rights, as a human being. In each case, one's rights are granted by being included in a certain group. So too, patients have rights by virtue of being included in that group of human beings called patients. They generally become patients by being accepted for care during and related to an illness by a physician, nurse and/or a hospital. In hospital nursing, a person usually becomes the patient of a nurse through the patient's relationship to the hospital. Both the American Hospital Association and the National League for Nursing have lists of patient's rights. The latter, entitled "Nursing's Role in Patient Rights," concludes with the statement, "Above all, patients have the right to be fully informed as to all their rights in all health care settings" (Saperstein and Frazier, 1980, p. 172). Certainly, this means that nurses should be the patient's advocate in the sense of informing them of their rights. In fact, the remaining stated rights imply that nurses should be advocates of patients' rights. When the nurse relates to the patient in an I-It (Thou) manner, she affirms that although this person is being treated impartially and therefore, impersonally, as a member of a group called patients, she recognizes that this patient is entitled to rightful treatment. Put differently, she treats the patient with the dignity and respect due a person, even when treating him impersonally.

Being Personal through Practice

Recognizing the rights of a patient gives her the respect due a person but does not establish a personal relationship with her. Developing such relationship would be rare indeed between nurse and patient if personal relationships required the unstructured relationships of friends and lovers. But responding in structured practice does not necessarily make the relationship impersonal. A personal relationship is one in which I respond to a particular person as he is present to me in ways which express my way of being with that person. For example, in taking the vital signs of a patient with terminal cancer, the nurse is asked by the patient if she knows how a mother can tell her son that she is dying. Then, a personal encounter should be called forth. Or, a nurse notices that a small child is very tense and nervous before her father's hernia operation and takes time to sit down and talk with the child in an assuring manner about the nature of the operation. Or, a surgical nurse, who after having been preoccupied with the routines during a difficult operation, compliments the surgeon on his quick thinking and his skillful execution of the surgery. Since so much of nursing is done on a routine basis, it is necessary for the nurse to be ready for a personal response whenever it is called for.

When I meet Thou, even in an initially impersonally structured relationship, I am in an I-Thou relationship. For example, when a nurse, in giving a routine injection, notices the tenseness and anxiety of her patient and responds with reassuring language and therapeutic touch which lessens the tension, thus reducing the pain of the injection, she is relating to the patient as I-Thou. In contrast, when a nurse gives an injection in a routinely prescribed manner with no personal response to the person receiving the injection, thereby giving a prescribed injection to "anybody," she is in an I-It relationship with the (not her) patient. Therefore, a nurse-patient relationship can be an I-Thou relationship, even when structured by the requirements of nursing practice. Nursing practice becomes a personal way of being when a nurse appropriates the practice of the profession in ways which express her way of being as nurse to this particular person as patient. Often appropriating nursing practice in personal ways is called expressing individuality. However, this is an unfortunate designation, since individuality is what sets us apart from a certain group. A nurse should act in particular ways as a nurse not in order to set himself apart from his colleagues but so that his unique way of being will contribute to a healing and fulfilling relationship with a particular patient.

Nurses who say they have no time for personal relationships with patients apparently believe that the personal relationships are dispensable, add-on requirements. For them, establishing personal relationships with patients is regarded as another moral imperative *in addition* to their regular professional duties. This separation of the personal from professional duties occurs when the personal is viewed as a moral imperative extrinsic to nursing practice and professional duties are regarded as intrinsic to practice. In professions like nursing, which have a dominant moral sense, one practices morality by thorough and conscientious practice. In fact, this is so much the case in nursing that nurses often practice without being explicitly aware of the moral sense of their practice. When one makes personal relations with patients a moral imperative in addition to nursing care, one assumes that personal relationships are merely another imperative for which one is responsible. In that case, a nurse is mainly responsible to the moral imperative to be related personally to the patient rather than being responsible to the patient. Then the patient is judged to have been treated morally when the nurse acts toward him under the imperative, "I ought to be personal with the patient."

Buber (1923/1970) helps us recognize the folly of applying such normative imperatives to personal relations by pointing out that the root of responsibility is responding. This, of course, means that one is primarily responsible to the person they meet as that person is present to them and not primarily to a moral principle under which the person is subsumed. Emanuel Levinas (1982/1985) carried Buber's approach to personal morality to its logical conclusion in his development of face-to-face relationships. For Levinas, meeting the person's face is what places the moral imperative for the good of the other on me. When I meet the other face-to-face, I encounter that which cannot be placed in space and time as a body-object. Meeting this otherness is the source of the moral imperative requiring radical responsibility for the other. Nurses certainly can appreciate what Levinas is talking about. One nurse in our study responded with moral indignation to the physician's transforming a ninety-one year old man, whose face looked like Harry S. Truman and radiated a "great sense of humor," into a body-object for the remaining ten days of his life during which he was "intubated, cardioverted, EP studied, hemodialized, B.P. maintained on cardiotonic drugs, etc." Another nurse who was "taking care of a stroke who was aphasic and had difficulty with ADL's," ceased treating the body-object when, while making his bed for the fourth time, she felt a touch and met a face which "smiled and so managed to say thank you." When we meet a patient face-to-face, we cannot regard that person as the body studied in anatomy class, to be known, manipulated and used. That face calls me to be responsible for the ill person I face as he is present to me.

The personal for the nurses in the foregoing examples was not a moral imperative, added to their duties, but the face that broke through their nursing routine and called forth a personal response. Often, nurses who say that personal relationships with patients should be avoided as nonprofessional, are hiding from the face of the patient who calls them from impersonal routine care into personal-professional responsibility. Nurses, who regard the most valuable aspect of the nurse-patient relationship as personal relationships, which have been added to nursing care as a bonus, have not met the face which integrates the professional with the personal.

Nurse and patient can cultivate a face-to-face relationship through dialogue. The leading interpreter of dialogue has been Buber, but his description of dialogue presupposes intimate I-Thou relationships. If nurses follow Buber's dyadic dialogue, then their primary relationship with patients would be intimate personal relationships, such as friendship. As John Macmurray (1978) points out, such intimate personal relationships have no end beyond themselves. The relationship is its own end. Friends and lovers are with each other simply because they enjoy being in each other's presence. A nurse, on the other hand, is rarely with a particular patient because they want to be with that patient as a person. In fact, she probably would rather be with her closest friend drinking coffee or in a canoe on a lake with her lover. Her relationship with her patient, in contrast, is based not on her desire to be with *that* particular person but to help that particular person to become well. Obviously, this relationship has an end beyond itself.

Triadic Dialogue

Since dialogue in the nurse-patient relationship has an end beyond itself, dialogue must be triadic, rather than dyadic. It is constituted not solely by the relationship of the partners as in Buber's dyadic dialogue but also by that which dialogue is about, i.e., the care of the patient. Triadic dialogue in education has been described by Scudder and Mickunas (1985) in a way which can be appropriated in nursing. Their description of triadic dialogue incorporates the personal I-Thou relationship into a dialogical relationship that has an end beyond itself. Educational dialogue is triadic in that the triad is formed by the two partners—teacher and student—focusing on that which is to be learned. Nurse and patient engage in dialogue focused on the well-being of the patient. In education and nursing the two partners are not equal in their understanding or skill in accomplishing the goal. Just as the teacher knows more about what is to be learned and how it is to be learned than the student, so the nurse almost always knows more about the illness being treated and how it needs to be treated than the patient. Just as the goal of teacher is to help his student acquire understanding and skill so that the student no longer needs him as a teacher, so the goal of the nurse is to help the patient become able to care for himself so that she is no longer needed. Although Buber's (1965, p. 100) dyadic conception of dialogue did allow for unequal understanding between the partners, it would not permit anything, such as something to be learned or the healing of a person, to be constitutive of the dialogue other than the partners themselves.

In triadic dialogue, the goal is different for nursing and education in two respects, however. First, nursing dialogue is not primarily aimed at understanding in the way that educational dialogue is. For example, a student cannot be said to have learned $2 + 2 = 4$ if he does not understand the meaning of four. The primary function of education is learning. One of the primary functions of nursing is also teaching and learning but nursing has other functions related to care for the ill. Put differently, nursing primarily aims at healing, but fostering healing usually requires the nurse to engage in dialogue with the patient concerning decisions related to his own treatment, care and future health. Second, unlike most educational dialogue, in which the two partners usually try to understand something in the world other than the partners, in nursing dialogue, the two partners discuss the condition and care of the partner who is the ill patient. After all, it is the patient's illness and treatment that is primarily under discussion. When the patient's illness is treated as disease, then her body is objectified as any body. Attending to the objectness of the person is more important in health care than in other practices concerned primarily with persons. In health care, practitioners are very much concerned with the body-object. If a person is ill, health care workers try to place that illness within the category of disease so that they will be able to cure or alleviate the disease. Generally this is done through standardized procedures, which means that the body is treated as anybody's body, thus as an object. This is why Gadow says that health care requires "attending to the 'objectness' of persons without reducing them to the moral status of objects" (Gadow, 1985, pp. 34–35). The need for dealing with people objectively without reducing them to an object, as we saw earlier, led Strasser (1985) to develop the concept of subject-object. Strasser, of course, was using this concept to deal with human activities like the practice of nursing. However, since the practice of nursing necessarily focuses on the human body as an object, there is often a tendency to deal with the patient as an object rather than as a subject with whom the nurse must discuss his body as an object.

Nurses, however, are not merely concerned with disease which requires objectification but also with illness which focuses on patients' experiences of illness. According to Benner and Wrubel (1989), one of the major responsibilities of the nurse is to help patients understand and anticipate their experience of illness and treatment. Illness and treatment often make patients' bodily responses foreign and not understandable (pp. 9–19). Nurses help patients to understand and anticipate these bodily changes. After all, they do not experience their bodies primarily as an object but as themselves.

Triadic dialogue, unlike dyadic dialogue, is uniquely suited to attending to the objectness of the person without reducing the person to the status of an object, and for understanding and anticipating the experience of illness and treatment. In triadic dialogue, the patient is talked with as a subject who is experiencing illness and treatment, even when attending to his body as an object. A nurse should help the patient understand his experience, drawing on her knowledge of medical science. But she also, from having lived through illness and treatment with other patients, should help the patient understand and live through his experience of illness. For example, a nurse is asked to follow up an explanation by a physician concerning why chemotherapy is necessary for his patient following surgery for cancer. The nurse is to discuss the side effects of the chemotherapy. But the nurse recognizes that what are referred to as side effects by the physician are personal effects to the patient. Accordingly, she speaks with the person who is her patient not about side effects but about the loss of her hair, the nausea and vomiting which she probably will experience, and her need to be careful because of an increased susceptibility to infection. A nurse, knowing how reluctant most patients are to directly face a colostomy, treats the irrigation of the colostomy in a very objective fashion. She speaks of the proper equipment and the amount of water to use for the irrigation and the cleaning of the stoma as if she were talking about caring for some piece of machinery. However, she talks to the patient about that machinery as a person with whom she is concerned and in such a way that the patient will learn how to care for it himself. She may even show the patient, his wife and other family members how to use humor as a means of accepting the surgical opening as his new rectum.

Triadic dialogue establishes what Alfred Schutz (1932/1967) calls a "we-relationship," in that we share an immediate space and time in a common world. Although some aspects of the we-relationship are mediated, the we-relationship is as close to an unmediated relationship as we humans have. In this relationship, we constitute a shared world even though we do not experience that world in exactly the same way. In one example given by Benner and Wrubel (1989), a nurse, through dialogue with a patient suffering from rheumatoid arthritis, was able to enter into that patient's world of pain and debilitation even though she had never experienced either immediately. The patient in response to the nurse's entering into her world said, " 'You know, no one has ever talked about it as a personal thing before, no one's ever talked to me as if this were a thing that mattered, a personal event' " (p. 11). In another case, a nurse so entered into a patient's experience of a mastectomy that the patient was astounded to discover that the nurse had not had a mastectomy herself (p. 13). These nurses could do this because they had lived through similar experiences with other patients in a we-relationship. Schutz describes such relations as follows:

> To this encounter with the other person I bring a whole stock of previously constituted knowledge. This includes both general knowledge of what another person is as such and any specific knowledge I may have of the person in question. It includes knowledge of other people's interpretive schemes, their habits, and their language. It includes knowledge of the taken-for-granted in-order-to and because-motives of others as such and of this person in particular. And when I am face to face with someone, my knowledge of him is increasing from moment to moment. My ideas of him undergo continuous revision as the concrete experience unfolds (Schutz, 1932/1967, p. 169).

Schutz contends that we-relationships are not experienced reflectively but as being lived through together.

> However, we must remember that the pure We-relationship, which is the very form of every encounter with another person, is not itself grasped *reflectively* within the face-to-face situation. Instead of being observed, it is lived through . . . Within the unity of this experience I can be aware simultaneously of what is going on in my mind and in yours, *living through* the two series of experiences as one series—what we are experiencing together (Schutz, 1932/1967, p. 170).

This unity by living through the experiences of patients is evident in two previous examples. The first is from a nurse working with a forty-three-year-old woman with metastatic cancer. "We cried together, laughed together, and conspired together to meet her needs even if it meant bending hospital policy." The second example, the statement of a patient who had a heart attack, describes his care as, "we were a team and this was a campaign. I was a member of the team. I was the cause of all the trouble but I was also a member of the team. We were holding hands" (Hardy, 1978, p. 209).

Although Schutz helps us grasp the meaning of we-re-relationships, his contention that we leave these relationships when we reflect on their meaning is questionable. Schutz, like Buber, believes that we-relationships are constituted only face to face. But in triadic dialogue the two partners face something in the world together, and therefore their we-relationship is side by side rather than face to face. From this side by side relationship, they can reflect on one partner's experience of illness or their relationship in living through that illness together and still remain in a we-relationship. Thus, the we-relationship can be maintained during reflection when we try to make sense of experiences and relationships which we live through together. This is very important to nurses, because they are usually the members of the health care team who help patients make sense of their experience of illness and treatment and of the relationships with health care professionals during these experiences.

Triadic dialogue is not only capable of making sense of a patient's experience and of the nurse-patient relationship but it is also well suited to the communicative action required in health care dialogue. Dialogue in a health care situation is not aimed primarily at understanding but at action to be taken with and on the patient in cooperation with health care professionals. For example, a patient complains to her nurse of feeling shaky, slightly nervous, and dizzy. The nurse, having just come on this shift, is unfamiliar with the case and had simply responded to the patient's call light. The nurse first explores the complaints of the patient by having the patient articulate more fully and explicitly what she is experiencing. The patient comments that she has on a few occasions had similar bodily feelings. The nurse knows that such feelings can come from hypoglycemia, but she also knows that these symptoms can result from insulin reaction. Since insulin reaction does require immediate action, she asks the patient for what she is being treated and then tells the patient she needs to go and find out about her medication. The nurse returns with a glass of orange juice for the patient to drink. The patient, being curious about the orange juice, asks for reasons for this odd medication. The nurse first explains that the orange juice will help restore the balance between the amount of insulin in the body and the sugar levels. Then she asks if anyone has explained the disease diabetes to her and the nature of her treatment. The patient says that her physician tried to explain it, but she could not understand some of his words and at the time of the brief explanation, she was very tired and distraught. The nurse explains diabetes, insulin trreatment, and insulin reactions to the patient dialogically, with the patient asking questions and volunteering her own experience of her body which led her to come to the hospital, experiences which she now recognizes as symptoms of diabetes. The patient also recounts her experience of insulin reaction; the nurse follows this with a description of the normally expected progression of insulin reaction which leads to shock if it goes untreated. She helps the patient recognize that the shakiness and dizziness which she just experienced are the beginning symptoms of an insulin raction and that eating a piece of candy or drinking a glass of orange juice will prevent her from developing more serious symptoms. After reassuring the patient that early response to the symptoms will usually prevent more serious consequences, she cautions the patient to seek help immediately if the other symptoms appear. Sensing that the patient is becoming tired, the nurse suggests that she return later to discuss the patient's illness and care. The patient says she thinks she will be able to recognize the early symptoms of insulin reaction and thanks the nurse for her clear and empathetic explanation. After graciously accepting the compliment, the nurse explains to the patient that she is the one who primarily must learn to care for herself as a diabetic and that she should learn as much about her own care as she can while she is still in the hospital. The nurse points out to the patient that she must learn to test her own urine for sugar; take extra precautions of cleanliness with her skin, particularly her feet; regulate her diet and exercise; and learn to give herself insulin injections. The nurse again offers to help the patient learn to care for herself. When the patient accepts her offer, the nurse also volunteers to talk with the dietician and the physician to work out a team approach for her learning to care for herself. She also suggests that she or others can help the patient's family to understand her condition and treatment.

The foregoing example focuses on the essence of triadic dialogue in nursing and at the same time manifests many significant components of dialogue. The essence of triadic dialogue is two subjects communicating about a common object. In our example the common object is first the changes the patient experiences in her own life which is treated as a subject-object. This subject-object is resignified into an object-object by the nurse who classifies it as symptoms of an insulin reaction. The purpose of this reclassification is not merely or primarily understanding, but action to be taken first by the nurse in restoring the insulin-sugar balance with the orange juice and later by the patient's learning to maintain and restore that balance herself. Thus, the nurse and patient are engaged in communicative action. This communicative action involves mutual sharing of experience and understanding. Some of the communication is educative in that the nurse possesses a superior understanding to that of the patient concerning diabetes and its treatment. The purpose of the educational dialogue is for the patient to come to a better understanding of diabetes and its treatment in terms of her own life and capabilities. The nurse, unlike the physician, translates medical knowledge into the everyday experience of the patient. In so doing, she is actually engaging in a hermeneutic spiral. The spiral begins with an articulation of the patient's experience; the theoretical understanding of the nurse is brought to bear on that experience so that the patient is better able to understand it. From this better understanding, the dialogue continues in further spirals directed toward the patient's decision to learn to care for herself in cooperation with the nurse and others. The nurse is more effective in helping the patient understand her illness and care because she was aware of the patient's condition during their dialogue, unlike the physician who talked on even though the patient was tired and distraught. Triadic dialogue requires that the partners be aware not only of the object under consideration but of their partner during the discussion. In addition, while the goal of health care dialogue is decision and action, both the decisions and the actions must be informed, hence, the need for communicative action. Communicative action becomes dialogical when the communication takes place between two subjects, not between one subject, the nurse, and an object, the patient. In dialogue, the two subjects (nurse and patient) discuss the patient's illness and care and her experience of them without reducing her to the status of an object.

Dialogue becomes triadic when intentionality is taken seriously. Intentionality, in phenomenological philosophy, means that we are not merely conscious but we are conscious of something or someone. This means that we don't just think, we think about something; we do not love, we love someone; we do not feel, we feel something. Further, this consciousness of something or someone occurs within horizons of meaning. In the foregoing example, the patient's horizon was her body as ordinarily experienced and articulated in everyday language. On the other hand, the nurse interpreted her experience through two related horizons. One horizon consisted of knowledge *of* patients drawn from descriptions of similar experiences by many of her patients; the other was medical knowledge about disease. Bringing the patient's experience into focus within these two horizons made it possible for her to understand the patient's experiences of her body as symptoms of insulin reaction. This nurse exemplifies one of the competencies of nursing; namely, the ability to relate the patient's experience of illness to medical knowledge of disease. The nurse's ability to do this prepared her patient to return to her everyday world with greater medical and experiential understanding of her chronic illness. By increasing the patient's horizons, the nurse prepared her for self-care, but the *way* in which the nurse engaged in dialogue with her patient encouraged and empowered her patient to care for herself.

Integral Language of Dialogue

In the foregoing example, the nurse is able to communicate effectively with the patient because she does so in integral language which involves the evocative, expressive and propositional modes of language. The physician in the foregoing illustration would probably attribute the lack of communication between himself and the patient as a typical example of the difficulty of trying to communicate the specialized, professional language of medicine to a patient. What he probably is unaware of is that the language of medicine is primarily propositional, which is the appropriate language for articulation of the natural sciences. For example, a physician might say to his patient following a mastectomy, "Eighty percent of your lymph nodes were involved with metastatic Ca and the treatment for this is only palliative." He has just told his patient that she will die in the near future in the language appropriate for telling someone that the motor of his car was beyond repair. In fact, a mechanic who knew that the owner really cared about his car would probably communicate in integral language rather than impersonal propositional language. Integral language is language in which three modes of language—the evocative, expressive, and propositional—are inseparably involved in communication.

Evocative Language

Evocative language calls forth a changed way of being in persons. Health care aims at bringing about a change in patients which we call healing. Healing usually requires a confident and positive attitude from the patient. Scott Peck (1978), a psychiatrist, calls this attitude the will to grow. He points out that his psychiatric patients who have a strong will to grow recover from a severe psychosis much more rapidly than patients with a mild neurosis who lack this will. A confident and positive attitude also fosters healing of patients who are physically ill, as Norman Cousins (1979) has shown. Certainly, this attitude is required in rehabilitation if the patient is to learn self-care in such everyday activities as getting out of bed and toileting while recovering from surgery or illness.

A nurse uses evocative language to say to the patient, "You can do it!" Of course, a nurse rarely says this directly. But since the nurse is usually the one who is in most continuous contact with the patient, she has ample opportunity for indirect communication. For example, a nurse may say to the patient directly, "If you are to be cured, you must do it yourself." But, the tone of her speech and the manner of her touch may say to the patient, "You alcoholics are hopeless and morally reprehensible because you can't control your lives." It is only when her speech and touch say to him, "You are an important, competent person," that she is saying indirectly to him, you can do it. The success of Alcoholics Anonymous in large part comes from a reformed alcoholic saying to an alcoholic directly and indirectly, "I did it, and you can do it too." Although most nurses probably have not personally experienced recovery from the same illness or debilitation their patients have, they often have lived through these experiences with other patients. Drawing on this experience and using evocative language in speech and touch, they can help patients to regain confidence in themselves.

Patients need encouragement and confidence to live through their illness, their confinement, their treatment and their participation in the healing process. When patients are encouraged through evocative language, they are enabled and empowered by speech and touch to recover the courage to be.

Expressive Language

Expressive language concerns our atunement to the world. In the case of nursing, this atunement is to the patient and to the practice which heals or alleviates his condition. In our previous discussion of an alcoholic patient, we gave an example of expressive as well as evocative language. When a nurse's language and touch conveys moral approbation and hopelessnes, she is expressing her feelings about the patient and the prognosis for curing his illness. Thus, expressive language is not expressing inner feelings but feelings about someone or something in the world. Sheila Orlick (1988) gives an excellent example of expressive language when she talks about a patient for whom she had cared for two months. She and the patient had developed a very close relationship. When the patient required additional surgery, he was transferred to Intensive Care and almost died. After he was returned to Orlick's care, he was uncharacteristically passive; his affect was flat; and he would not make eye contact with her. She explains:

> I tried various therapeutic interventions that I had learned in nursing school to get him to talk about his feelings, but all he would do was nod his head or stare blankly at the wall. Finally, I said to him: "You just don't care any more, do you?" All he did was shake his head. At that point my emotions "got the best of me." I had been working with this man for two months, knew his family, and had developed a relationship with him. I felt he was shutting me out and it made me feel sad, frustrated, and angry all at once. At that moment, all the therapeutic nursing intervention strategies I had learned just left me. I responded to Gerald on a gut level. I yelled at him, "Well damn it, Gerald, *we* care!" (pp. 318–319).

Upset by her outburst, Orlick left the room. When she returned about an hour later, Gerald was crying. When she asked him if he was O.K., he reached for her hand, squeezed it, and said, "Thank you."

In contrast to Sheila Orlick, who used expressive language so forcefully and appropriately, some nurses seem to exude love for everyone but fail to express love through concrete care for anyone. Nurses who have a vague positive attitude concerning everything usually convey to their patients that they do not really grasp the meaning of their situation. A patient who is dying of terminal cancer is repelled by nurses who assure her that everything will come out all right. The nurse cannot honestly give such assurance, but she can assure her patient of her concern by her empathic touch and speech. Such expression of concern is most meaningful when it conveys a shared atunement between nurse and patient, as in the previously mentioned case of the most fulfilling experience of one nurse. After the death of her forty-one-year-old patient with metastatic cancer, she described this atunement as follows: "We cried together, laughed together, and conspired together to meet her needs even if it meant bending hospital policy" (Scudder and Bishop, 1986, p. 149).

In such shared atunement both partners experience each other as subjects. In contrast, when both nurse and patient assume an exclusively medical stance, they relate to each other as objects. Then the patient's body becomes an object to be probed, measured, and tested. In this I-It relationship the nurse's body also becomes the instrument for the probing, the measuring and the testing. Gadow (1985) calls this technological touch. (Later, we will treat this as propositional language.) With this "neutral" technological touch, Gadow contrasts philanthropic touch which reduces the patient to an object on which benefits are bestowed. She compares technological and philanthropical touch with empathetic touch.

> In the caring relationship, the body is regarded—and touched—by the nurse as the immediate, lived reality of the patient. This entails a breach of objectivity: empathic touch affirms, rather than ignores, the subjective significance of the body for the patient. Its purpose is not palpation or manipulation but expression—an expression of the nurse's participation in the patient's experience. Because subjective involvement in another's suffering is possible only where concern exists, empathic touch is concern made tangible (Gadow, 1985, pp. 40–41).

Empathetic touch does not express the presumption that the nurse knows what it is to suffer and fear as the patient does. Instead, it assures the patient that the nurse is caring for him because she really cares for him. Thus, she expresses to the patient what Richard Zaner says that every patient wants most to know: "That those who care for him, really care for him" (Zaner, 1985, p. 96).

Propositional Language

Gadow's technological touch is hardly neutral with regard to relating to the patient as subject or object. It may be neutral in that it does not actively demean or affirm the patient, as she claims. But since it is propositional, it does treat the patient as an object among objects. In Buber's poetic treatment of I-It relationships, the patient becomes, "a dot in the world grid of space and time" (Buber, 1923/1970, p. 59). In nursing one does this by relating to the patient as a typical case of disease X, or as needing some procedure to be carried out by the book, or as an obstinate patient who needs to conform to hospital routine. Put positively, the nurse looks for typical symptoms which will help the physician in diagnosis and treatment, uses time-tested procedures to minimize suffering and enhance healing, and promotes smooth and efficient patient care through time-tested hospital procedures. But regardless of whether stated positively or negatively, propositional language always regards the patient as an object. Therefore, it is not neutral concerning whether the patient is to be treated as subject or object. It follows the propositional deployment of the world, which dictates that if we use procedure X, then Y will result; that patient treatment should follow a routine, clock-ordered time; that patients are to be put into categories on the basis of their disease (not illness) and treated according to prescribed medical procedures.

Our point is certainly not that relating to patients through evocative and expressive language is good and relating to them through propositional language is bad. The use of propositional language is necessary in medical diagnosis, treatment, and prognosis. When a patient asks a nurse about the medical aspects of his diagnosis, treatment or prognosis, the nurse certainly must be able to think propositionally to give an answer. Further, the translation of this information from medical language to everyday language does not alter the fact that it is propositional language. For example, if a tennis buff asks his nurse after a major heart attack whether he can resume playing tennis, and she replies, "No, because vigorous exercise will probably further damage your heart," this is a translation from theoretical propositional language into everyday propositional language. If she had articulated it in medical language, she would have stated that because of the continued restriction in the arteries which provoked the heart attack and the destruction of the tissue by the heart attack, the heart will not have sufficient oxygen to adjust to vigorous exercise. Her statement in either everyday or professional language is propositional language, since it employs an if-then logic and draws on her knowledge of the functioning of any heart.

Obviously, health care requires the use of propositional language. Indeed, medical knowledge and treatment are appropriately articulated in propositional language regardless of whether it is the professional language used between the nurse and physician or the everyday language between nurse and patient. Propositional language is not neutral; it does treat the patient as an object. But as Gadow (1985) puts it, health care requires "attending to the 'objectness' of persons without reducing them to the moral status of objects" (pp. 33–34).

Integral Language

One way in which patients are turned into objects is through using *only* propositional language. When the aforementioned tennis buff is answered by his nurse with the if-then logic of propositional language, her language is inappropriate, because he is not inquiring about doing a certain type of physical activity but about the possibility of his *being* a tennis player again. Such possibilities cannot be de-

scribed in the way one assesses a piece of machinery for fulfilling a specific function. The possibility of being a tennis
player raises the issue of the meaning of tennis to that person called her patient. Does he mean by playing tennis
being a "serious" player in tournaments or simply one who
plays for enjoyment? Whether either are possible in the future depends upon his recovery and his attitude concerning
his illness and himself as a tennis player. Such possibilities
and attitudes cannot be expressed in propositional language. Propositional language, however, can state prognosis
which is essential in assessing possible recovery or improvement. But prognosis is stated within the limits of medical
treatment which eliminates other intervening factors. But
such other factors as attitudes and life styles do intervene.
Some of these intervening factors do foster healing. Therefore, when nurses discuss possibilities for recovery and a
good life, they should do so in integral language which
unites the evocative, expressive and propositional into a
common language capable of articulating all aspects of
human being and becoming.

The way nurses actually talk *in* practice is more appropriate than the way they talk *about* practice. Nurses tend to
communicate with their patients in integral language. For
example, the nurse may describe the treatment of a patient's
disease propositionally while holding his hand in a way that
conveys her concern for him and gives him assurance that
the treatment will improve his condition. Or she may describe propositionally the time-tested procedure for getting
out of bed after a certain kind of surgery, knowing that if he
does it in this way, it will minimize pain and reduce the
chance of injury. At the same time, her words and touch assure him that she knows of and cares about the pain he will
experience. Her calming speech and gentle but firm assistance in helping him from the bed expresses her care concretely. Further, her confident tone assures him that he soon
will be able to do this for himself.

Although most nurses tend to use integral language in
communicating with their patients, the increase in science,
technology and professionalism in health care inclines

them to regard propositional language as the language for health care. When they articulate their practice, it usually is done in propositional language. Neophytes in nursing schools are instructed primarily in propositional language. Yet when nurses actually practice, they communicate with their patients mostly in integral language. What is needed is an articulation of the language of nursing, as practiced, rather than as articulated propositionally in talk about the discipline of nursing. Most nurses use integral language because practice requires it. They need to understand the meaning of integral language and how to use it to communicate with each other concerning nursing itself.

Alternation of Dominance

Although nursing practice requires the use of integral language, the mode which is dominant at any particular time ought to be appropriate to the patient, the medical condition and the situation. For example, if one were trying to decide between two alternative medical treatments, he would presumably want the nurse to speak to him primarily in propositional language. Thus, propositional, rather than evocative or expressive language, would be focal. On the other hand, a person being moved to the operating room for a delicate and dangerous operation would not want the nurse to explain the technicalities of the operation but instead would welcome assurance and personal caring. This implies that in integral language one dimension of language is more appropriate than others for a particular situation and that this dimension should be dominant. Thus, there is in integral language what Alfred North Whitehead (1967) calls an "alternation of dominance" (p. 28). In other words, in any nurse-patient relationship, either expressive, evocative, or propositional language will be called forth as the dominant language, according to the patient care situation. Further, the non-dominant dimensions are always potentially dominant as the situation calls for it.

The actual language used in nursing practice is more integral than is supposed by the proponents of "scientific nursing." Indeed, clearer articulation of the nature of integral language actually used in practice should improve the communication between practitioners and their patients and challenge the privileged status of propositional language being imposed on nursing care in the name of science. After all, it is the inclusion of expressive and evocative language in communication between nurse and patient which expresses and evokes the personal in their relationship.

Chapter 9

Conclusion

We shall not cease from exploration
And the end of all our exploring
Will be to arrive where we started
And know the place for the first time

(T. S Eliot, 1943, p 39).

Nursing is a practice with its own legitimate authority and its own unique in-between situation. It is a practice which is founded on the moral imperative to foster the physical and psychological well-being of persons, especially when ill, by caring for them in personal relationships. With these statements, "at the end of our exploring," we have arrived where we started. But to recognize the place for the very first time calls for a retracing of our path from the end to the beginning.

We concluded our exploration by examining the personal relationship between nurse and patient. We will retrace our exploration of the essence of nursing from the personal sense with which we concluded back through the moral sense on which it is founded, to the practical sense with which we began.

The personal relationship between patient and nurse requires the use of integral language. Exclusive use of propositional language, without evocative and expressive language, fosters impersonal relationships. Sometimes nursing practice requires treating patients impersonally for reasons such as establishing distance between nurse and patient.

But even in these relationships, nurses should treat patients with the dignity and respect due persons. We have called this relationship an I-It (Thou) relationship. In such relationships, nurses should be open to personal encounter with the person for whom they are caring. The primary relationship between nurse and patient is an I-Thou relationship. Such relationships are usually triadic rather than dyadic because the relationship has an end beyond itself which requires the nurse and patient to work together to foster the well-being of the patient. Also, authentic nursing is personal in the sense that nurses express their personal way of being through the way in which they appropriate nursing practice in relationship to the particular person they encounter as patient.

Fostering the well-being of the patient requires the cooperation of nurses, patients, physicians, hospital bureaucrats, and others in communal team relationships. For this reason the nurse's traditional in-between situation affords her a privileged position from which to foster team decisions utilizing the legitimate authority of all team members in the plan of mutual care for the patient. To this cooperative team effort, the nurse also contributes her expertise concerning day to day patient care.

Exercising this legitimate authority is different from acting autonomously. Legitimate authority designates an area of primary responsibility for care rather than one in which decisions are made unilaterally. The excessive desire for autonomy for nurses, as well as for other health care professionals, ignores the cooperation required by health care. Often the demand for autonomy is imported into nursing from philosophical ethics where it is regarded as a necessary condition for making moral decisions based on traditional moral norms. Although the norms and procedures of traditional philosophical ethics are helpful to nurses in making moral decisions concerning patient care, they cannot be used to structure that care without distorting its essential nature. An appropriate nursing ethic is a clinical ethic which comes from within nursing practice rather than being imposed from without.

A clinical ethic is appropriate for nursing because nursing is constituted by a moral sense inherent in its practice. For this reason, the primary moral responsibility of the nurse is excellent practice. Moral problems and dilemmas occur within practice itself rather than being imposed from outside practice by such factors as advancements in medical science and technology. Such advancements merely intensify and magnify moral problems already inherent in practice. These problems appear when the moral sense of practice is frustrated or inhibited, for example, when the different intentionalities in specialized practice lose sight of the cooperation needed to foster the well-being of patients; when maintaining distance from patients prevents nurses from being personally accessible to them; and when the desire to keep a stable nursing practice inhibits attempts to reform practice by realizing the possibilities for good inherent in it. Since nursing has an intrinsic moral sense, an ethic of practice is required rather than an applied ethic.

The moral sense is the dominant sense of nursing practice. Nurses find fulfillment when concrete patient care contributes to the well-being of patients and especially when appreciation for good care is personally expressed by patients. Professional and technical accomplishment becomes important when, rather than being ends in themselves, they contribute to the well-being of patients by preventing complications and fostering patient progress. Thus, nurses find fulfillment when nursing competency in a practice achieves the concrete good for the patient in a way which confirms the worth of that practice and of the nurse herself. But this confirmation is most deeply felt when the excellent care eventuates in an appreciative personal relationship between nurse and patient.

Since nursing is constituted by a moral sense, competency and virtue are integrally related. Competency names what excellent nurses do, virtue what nurses must be in order to do what they do. For this reason, Benner's nursing competencies can easily be translated into virtues. Practice *is* a union of being and doing. As Gadamer and MacIntyre pointed out, this union is not primarily an individual ac-

complishment but a corporate achievement by those who
constitute and contribute to a practice. True practices,
while historically developed, are never static but are always
dynamic in that they continually try to realize the possibilities inherent in traditional practice. They appreciate
and continue tradition but in ways that move practice for-
ward toward what it ought to become.

For practices such as nursing to progress, they must be
studied in ways appropriate to the practice itself. Thus, the
sense of nursing should be articulated by the human sciences because nursing practice is a human achievement
which fosters human well-being through a special caring relationship between nurse and patient. Therefore, although
nursing uses natural and social science, nursing itself cannot be adequately understood as applied science. Applied
science degenerates practice into mere technique, whereas
the human sciences articulate nursing as practiced. In so
doing, they avoid the separation of theory and practice
which results from applying theories drawn from outside
nursing to nursing practice.

The human sciences, especially through the hermeneutic spiral, make it possible to incorporate the natural sciences into the study of health care practice without making
it into an applied science. In this way, the spectacular advances in cure can be incorporated into health care without
making it health cure. Health care, after all, begins not with
disease but with illness which prevents persons from living
as they are accustomed to being or as they desire to be. The
health care relationship is initiated when the ill person
seeks the help of physician and nurse. This relationship is
established when physician and nurse profess to be competent to give that help by using their skill and understanding
to promote the patient's well-being in ways acceptable to
the patient. Thus, health care includes Pellegrino's four
senses of care: care as compassion; care as doing for others
what they cannot do for themselves; care as using competent skill and understanding; and care as taking care.

We have now "arrived where we started" with the essence of nursing. Now it is time to see if we "know the

place for the first time" (Eliot, 1943). Nursing is a major health care practice which can be distinguished from other health care practices. Nursing is a practice in that it is an ordered way of caring for the ill developed over time. But it is not a static or stagnant practice but one which, by realizing possibilities inherent within it, is growing and evolving in response to its enduring meaning and to changes in general health care and in society. As nursing has developed, two primary practical senses of nursing are discernable. The first sense comes from articulating the day-by-day care in which nurses exercise their own legitimate authority, as Benner has done with nursing competencies. The second sense is what we have described as the in-between relationship in which nurses work in-between physicians, hospital bureaucrats and patients to foster cooperative care for the ill. The two practical senses of nursing are concrete expressions of the moral sense which founds nursing practice and structures it so as to foster the physical and psychological well-being of persons. Articulation of how this good is accomplished through practice brings to consciousness the moral sense of nursing. The moral sense is actually realized through a personal relationship between nurse and patient. This personal relationship has three dominant senses: the first calls for establishing a dialogical relationship which is triadic since the relationship has an end beyond itself; the second for treating the patient with the dignity and worth due a person; and the third for expressing through nursing practice a nurse's personal response to a particular patient.

If we have adequately described the essence of nursing practice, nurses who have followed to "the end of all our exploring" will not say "Now for the first time we know what nursing really is," but instead, they will say with a deepened sense of recognition, "Oh, we haven't thought of it that way, but we've always known that!" Thus, they will be able to truly say with T. S. Eliot (1943),

> And the end of all our exploring
> Will be to arrive where we started
> And know the place for the very first time.

The purpose of phenomenological analysis is to bring to consciousness what we already know from practice but have not yet articulated, rather than to develop new and novel ways of understanding and engaging in practice. This bringing to consciousness improves practice directly by fostering enlightenment. Phenomenological philosophy of nursing further contributes an articulation of the practical sense of nursing by bringing to consciousness the essence of nursing practice within the moral and personal web of meaning which that practice, itself, presupposes. It fosters improvement in nursing by raising to consciousness possibilities for excellent practice in ways that encourage their realization by practitioners. Thus, improvement of nursing does not come from philosophers or other outside "experts" prescribing new practice, but from nurses themselves actually recognizing and realizing the possibilities inherent in their practice, thus contributing to a living dynamic practice directed toward the future.

References

Aydelotte, M. (1984). Foreward. In P. Benner, *From novice to expert* (pp. v–vii). Menlo Park, CA: Addison-Wesley.

American Nurses' Association. (1980). *Nursing: A social policy statement*. Kansas City, MO: Author.

Aristotle. Nicomachean ethics. Translated by W. D. Ross. In McKeon, R. (ed.). (1941). *The Basic Work of Aristotle*. New York: Random House.

Aroskar, M. (1985). Ethical relationships between nurses and physicians: Goals and realities—A nursing perspective. In A. Bishop and J. R. Scudder Jr. (eds.), *Caring, curing, coping: Nurse, physician, patient relationships* (pp. 44–61). University, AL: University of Alabama Press.

Barritt, L. S., Beekman, T., Bleeker, H., & Mulderij, K. (1983). *A handbook for phenomenological research in education*. Ann Arbor: University of Michigan.

Benner, P. (1984). *From novice to expert: Excellence and power in clinical nursing practice*. Menlo Park, CA: Addison-Wesley.

Benner, P. & Wrubel, J. (1989). *The primacy of caring: Stress and coping in health and disease*. Menlo Park, CA: Addison-Wesley.

Buber, M. (1958). *I and Thou* (2nd ed.) (R. G. Smith, trans.) New York: Charles Scribner's Sons. (Original work published c. 1923).

Buber, M. (1965). *Between man and man*. (R. G. Smith, trans.). New York: Macmillan. (Original work published 1926–1939).

Buber, M. (1970). *I and Thou* (W. Kaufmann, trans.). New York: Charles Scribner's Sons. (Original work published c. 1923).

Cassell, E. J. (1988). Foreword: Progress in Ethics. in Zaner, R. *Ethics and the clinical encounter.* Englewood Cliffs, N.J.: Prentice-Hall.

Cousins, N. (1979). *Anatomy of an illness as perceived by the patient.* Toronto: Bantam Books.

Eliot, T. S. (1943). "Little Gidding." In *Four Quartets.* (pp. 31–39). New York: Harcourt, Brace.

Engelhardt, H. T., Jr. (1982). Illnesses, diseases, and sicknesses. In V. Kestenbaum (ed.). *The humanity of the ill* (pp. 142–156). Knoxville: University of Tennessee Press.

Engelhardt, H. T., Jr. (1985) Physicians, patients, health care institutions—and the people in between: nurses. In A. H. Bishop and J. R. Scudder, Jr. (eds.). *Caring, curing, coping: Nurse, physician, patient relationships* (pp. 62–79). University, AL: University of Alabama Press.

Fry, S. (1986). Ethical aspects of decision-making in the feeding of cancer patients. *Seminars in Oncology Nursing* 2 (1), p. 59–62.

Gadamer, H. G. (1981). *Reason in the age of science* (F. G. Lawrence, trans.). Cambridge, MA: MIT Press. (Original work published 1976).

Gadow, S. (1980). Existential advocacy: Philosophical foundation of nursing. In S. Spicker and S. Gadow (eds.). *Nursing: Images and ideals: Opening dialogue with the humanities* (pp. 79–101). New York: Springer.

Gadow, S. (1982). Body and self: A dialectic. In V. Kestenbaum (ed.). *The humanity of the ill* (pp. 86–100). Knoxville: University of Tennessee Press.

Gadow, S. (1985). Nurse and patient: The caring relationship. In A. H. Bishop and J. R. Scudder, Jr. (eds.), *Caring, curing, coping: Nurse, physician, patient relationships.* University, AL: University of Alabama Press.

Gebser, J. (1985). The ever-present origin. (N. Barstad with A. Mickunas, trans.). Athens, OH: Ohio University Press. (Original work published 1949).

Gilligan, C. (1982). *In a different voice: Psychological theory and women's development.* Cambridge, MA: Harvard University Press.

Hardy, R. C. (1978). Sick: How people feel about being sick and what they think of those who care for them. Chicago: Teach 'em, Inc.

Hauerwas, S. (1986). *Suffering presence.* Notre Dame: University of Notre Dame Press.

Haworth, L. (1986). *Autonomy.* New Haven: Yale University Press.

Heidegger, M. (1962). *Being and time* (J. Macquarrie & E. Robinson, trans.). New York: Harper and Row.

Heidegger, M. (1966). *Discourse on thinking* (J. M. Anderson and E. H. Freund, trans.) New York: Harper & Row. (Original work published 1959).

Hoy, D. C. (1978). *The critical circle: Literature, history, and philosophical hermeneutics.* Berkeley: University of California Press.

Hume, D. (1965). Dialogues concerning natural religion. In R. Cohen (ed.). *Essential works of David Hume.* New York: Bantam.

Husserl, E. (1965). *Phenomenology and the crisis of philosophy.* (Q. Lauer, trans.). New York: Harper & Row. (Original work published 1911).

James, W. (1948). The moral philosopher and the moral life. In A. Castell (ed). *Essays in pragmatism.* New York: Hafner Press.

Johnson, B. S. (1986). *Psychiatric-mental health nursing: Adaptation and growth.* Philadelphia: Lippincott.

Kesey, K. (1973). *One Flew Over the Cuckoo's Nest.* New York: Viking.

Kestenbaum, V. (1982). Introduction: The experience of illness. In V. Kestenbaum (Ed.). *The humanity of the ill.* (pp. 3–38). Knoxville: University of Tennessee Press.

Koch, Donald, Moral philosophers and moral expertise. *Philosophy and Medicine Newsletter:* Fall 1986: 2–3.

Kuhn, T. S. (1970). *The structure of scientific revolutions.* (2nd ed.). Chicago: University of Chicago Press.

Levinas, E. (1985). *Ethics and infinity*. (R. A. Cohen, trans.). Pittsburgh: Duquesne University Press. (Original work published 1982).

MacIntyre, A. (1984). *After virtue*. (2nd ed.). Notre Dame, IN: University of Notre Dame Press.

Macmurray, J. (1978). *Reason and emotion*. Atlantic Highlands, NJ: Humanities Press.

Mendelsohn, R. S. (1978). Foreword. In R. C. Hardy, *Sick: How people feel about being sick and what they think of those who care for them*. Chicago: Teach 'Em Press.

Merleau-Ponty, M. (1962). *Phenomenology of perception*. (C. Smith, trans.). London: Routledge & Kegan Paul.

Newman, B. (1982). *The Neuman systems model: Application to nursing education and practice*. Norwalk, CT: Appleton-Century-Crofts.

Nightingale, F. (1946). *Notes on nursing*. Philadelphia: Edward Stern. (Original work published in 1859).

Noddings, N. (1984). *Caring: A feminine approach to ethics and moral education*. Berkeley: University of California Press.

Orem, D. (1980). *Nursing: Concepts of practice* (2nd ed.). New York: McGraw-Hill.

Orlick, S. (1988). The primacy of caring. *American Journal of Nursing, 88*, pp. 318–319.

Peck, M. S. (1978). *The road less traveled*. New York: Simon and Schuster.

Pellegrino, E. (1982). Being ill and being healed. In V. Kestenbaum (ed.). *The humanity of the ill* (pp. 157–166). Knoxville: University of Tennessee Press.

Pellegrino, E. (1985). The caring ethic. In A. H. Bishop and J. R. Scudder, Jr. (eds.). *Caring, curing, coping: Nurse, physician, patient relationships* (pp. 8–30). University, AL: University of Alabama Press.

Polkinghorne, D. E. (1983). *Methodology for the human sciences: Systems of inquiry*. Albany: State University of New York Press.

Rawlinson, M. C. (1982). Medicine's discourse and the practice of medicine. In V. Kestenbaum (ed.). *The humanity of the ill* (pp. 69–85). Knoxville: University of Tennessee Press.

Ricoeur, P. (1965). *History and truth* (C.A. Kelbley, trans.). Evanston, IL: Northwestern University Press.

Ricoeur, P. (1977). Phenomenology and the social sciences. In M. Korenbaum (ed.). *The annals of phenomenological sociology II* (pp. 145–159). Dayton, OH: Wright State University.

Rosenberg, C. E. (1979). Florence Nightingale on contagion: The hospital as moral universe. In C. C. Rosenberg (ed.). *Healing and history* (pp. 116–136). New York: Dawson Science History Publications.

Saperstein, A. B., and Frazier, M. A. (1980). *Introduction to nursing practice*. Philadelphia: F. A. Davis.

Schrag, C. O. (1986). *Communicative praxis and the space of subjectivity*. Bloomington: Indiana University Press.

Schutz, A. (1967). *The Phenomenology of the social world*. (G. Walsh and F. Lehnert, trans.). Chicago: Northwestern University Press. (Original work published 1932).

Scudder, J. R. and Bishop, A. H. (1986). The moral sense and health care. In A-T. Tymieniecka (ed.) *Moral sense in the communal significance of life, Analecta Husserliana 20* (pp. 125–158). Dordrecht-Boston: D. Reidel.

Scudder, J. R., and Mickunas, A. (1985). *Meaning, dialogue, and enculturation: Phenomenological philosophy of education*. Washington, DC: Center for Advanced Research in Phenomenology and University Press of America.

Sharkey, P. (1986, Fall). There is no acme in ethical consulting. *Philosophy and Medicine Newsletter*, p. 7.

Sheard, T. (1980). The structure of conflict in nurse-physician relations. *Supervisor Nurse 11*, (pp. 14–15, 17–18).

Smith, H. (1965). *Condemned to meaning*. New York: Harper and Row.

Strasser, S. (1985). *Understanding and explanation: Basic ideas concerning the humanity of the human sciences*. Pittsburgh: Duquesne University Press.

Tisdale, S. (1986). *The sorcerer's apprentice: Inside the mod-*

ern hospital. New York: McGraw-Hill.

Toulmin, S. (1982). How medicine saved the life of ethics. *Perspectives in Biology and Medicine, 25,* pp. 736–750.

Tuma v. Board of Nursing of State of Idaho, 100 Idaho 74, 593 P. 2d 711 (1979).

Tymieniecka, A. T. (1983). The moral sense. In A. T. Tymieniecka and C. O. Schrag (eds.). *Foundations of morality, human rights, and the human sciences: Phenomenology in a foundational dialogue with the human sciences, Analecta Husserliana 15.* Dordrecht-Boston: D. Riedel.

Tymieniecka, A. T. (1984, May). *The moral sense in the phenomenological praxeology of the human science.* Paper presented at the meeting of the Third Annual Human Science Conference, West Georgia College.

Whitehead, A. N. (1967). *Aims of education.* New York: Free Press.

Woodham-Smith, C. (1983). *Florence Nightingale: 1820–1910.* New York: Atheneum.

Yarling, R. R., and McElmurry, B. (1986). The moral foundation of nursing. *Advances in Nursing Science 8* (2) pp. 63–73.

Zaner, R. M. (1985). "How the hell did I get here?" Reflections on being a patient. In A. H. Bishop and J. R. Scudder (eds.). *Caring, curing, coping: Nurse, physician, patient relationships.* University, AL: University of Alabama Press.

Zaner, R. M. (1988). *Ethics and the clinical encounter.* Englewood Cliffs, NJ: Prentice–Hall.

Index